The Devotional Life of a Pastor's Wife

Volume 3

By Various Authors

Copyright © November 2021. Revised edition, Volume 3 by Charlotte Claxton and other authors.

All rights reserved. No parts of this book may be reproduced or used in any manner without written permission of the copyright owner except for the use of quotations in a book review.

All scripture quotations, unless otherwise indicated, are taken from the Holy Bible. All rights reserved worldwide.

Scripture quotations marked (NKJV) are taken from New King James Version®. Copyright © 1982 by Thomas Nelson. Used by permission.

Scripture quotations marked (NIV) are taken from NEW INTERNATIONAL VERSION®, NIV® Copyright © 1973, 1978, 1984, 2011 by Biblica, Inc.® Used by permission.

Scripture quotations marked (MESS) are takes from *THE MESSAGE*, copyright © 1993, 2002, 2018 by Eugene H. Peterson. Used by permission of NavPress. All rights reserved. Represented by Tyndale House Publishers, Inc.

Scripture quotations marked (ESV) are taken from The ESV® Bible (The Holy Bible, English Standard Version®). ESV® Text Edition: 2016. Copyright © 2001 by Crossway, a publishing ministry of Good News Publishers. The ESV® text has been reproduced in cooperation with and by permission of Good News Publishers. Unauthorized reproduction of this publication is prohibited. All rights reserved.

All Scripture quotations marked (AMP) are taken from the Amplified Bible, Copyright © 2015 by The Lockman Foundation. Used by permission.

All quotations and definitions taken from another source have been clearly indicated and referenced in the appendix at the back of the book.

Exterior cover design by Natalie Decosta

Printed material by Frame Vector created by BiZkettE1 Freepik.com. This cover has been designed using resources from Freepik.com

Interior page design by Natalie Decosta and Sophie Holt.

Each testimony and story are true. To maintain anonymity some minor details have been changed.

The Devotional Life of a Pastor's Wife project lead by Charlotte Claxton. Foreword by Anonymous

Other authors include: Chantella Claxton, Sophie Holt, Hannah Sekimpi, Hannah Crisp, Natalie Decosta, Linda Temple, Claire Mabey, Maria Brick, Hollie Galt, Penny Boddy, Patricia Wainaina, Jacqui Wilkie, Heather Rice, Joanne Dale, Ombline Amponsa

ISBN: 9798502251419

THIS BOOK BELONGS TO

....

....

For every woman who was, is or desires to be the wife of a pastor

Our prayer is that this book will further equip you as a Christian and cause you to fall in love with Jesus more and more.

ACKNOWLEDGEMENTS

The Team aka 'The Armour Bearers'
Each of the following women were a part of the original WhatsApp group that inspired this book, without them this book would not have been possible. Every task that has been delegated to them has been fully embraced and efficiently completed, they have never let me down. Every devotion they have contributed has and will cause the reader to feel encouraged, challenged and inspired. Together we have fasted and prayed that this book would bless and revolutionise the life of a pastor's wife.

Chantella Claxton: Thank you for your consistency, words of encouragement and fantastic administrative skills.

Hannah Sekimpi: Thank you for your unwavering support, your time in formatting the manuscript and for your care of other pastor's wives.

Hannah Crisp: Thank you for being a listening ear and for making me laugh.

Natalie Decosta: Thank you for your tireless efforts on the design of the book; your skills have been paramount in this project. You are the reason it looks so beautiful. Thank you.

Sophie Holt: Thank you for the gorgeous artwork you contributed to the internal pages of the book. Thank you for picking up the phone (mostly late at night) when I couldn't contain my excitement about a new idea, devotion or when I had a question that I couldn't answer.

I thank everyone one of you for your friendship.

Doctrinal proof-readers
Pastor Daniel Crisp, Pastor Sam Holt, Pastor Adam Claxton, Pastor Lewis Claxton

These men willingly took on the important challenge of checking every devotion and testimony to make sure that every scripture fitted the thought. A time-consuming task on top of all that is required of them nevertheless they did it. Thank you.

Editors
Trisha Malone: A wonderful, faithful woman who desired to glorify God by willingly taking on the mammoth task of editing the 261 devotions and 52 testimonies. Although she had never edited before the team and I believed she possessed the skills to do it. We approached her and she at that point (during

Covid19) had been praying for the Lord to open a door for her to do something for Him; this was her answered prayer. God is good. She has been efficient and hard working. Thank you.

David Drum: David has been instrumental in the completion of this project; his editing skills have added the sleek touch to each devotion and testimony. We are so grateful for your lastminute.com interventions; they are remarkable. Thank you.

Proof-readers
Delphine Mensah and Cheryl Nembhard: Thank you for your diligent efforts in putting this book through the refining process. You've done a beautiful job.

Other
On behalf of myself and the team, we want to thank our families. Thank you for your love and prayers. There have been many periods during this amazing project when our minds and time have been consumed however you have been patient and released us. We thank God for you and love you to the ends of the earth.

Pastor Paul Boddy: For your support during this book and thank you for trusting us to do it.

INTRODUCTION

Hello, my name is Charlotte Claxton. I am a Christian, a mother, and a pastor's wife.

Who knew that 2020 would be a year that could change life as we know it, potentially for ever! I want to tell you a little about how the Coronavirus pandemic has changed my life and the lives of other pastor's wives around me, thus inspiring this book.

The rumours that the UK was going into lockdown were spreading around mid-February. If I'm honest (although I wished the circumstances weren't so horrific) I couldn't wait, I love being with my family. As I began to prepare for lockdown, stockpiling toilet paper (just kidding), school supplies and food, I pondered how this pandemic would affect our church. I considered the different circumstances the people in our congregation were living and dealing with (some with mental health issues, underlying health conditions, nurses, doctors, elderly, single mums, new converts) and wondered how was this going to affect them. *How was I going to engage with the ladies for potentially months? More importantly, how could I help them maintain a spiritual mindset and encourage them to stay focused on the Word and prayer?* The love I have for these ladies drove me to prayer, 'Lord you have to show me what to do.'

The Holy Spirit inspired me to invite the ladies to participate in posting a devotion on our WhatsApp group. I challenged them to use a scripture from their daily bible reading, write a thought to accompany it, and a prayer at the end if they felt necessary. It was a worthy shot in the dark if it meant we could all stay connected with each other and to Jesus. To my amazement, sixteen women responded. Words cannot express how insightful, encouraging, and motivating it was to read their devotions every morning during a pandemic; God used every one of them.

My mind also turned to pioneer churches, mainly pastor's wives. A church that is not yet established with core families and individuals could be detrimentally affected in a time like this. 'Goodness,' I thought, 'they're going to need a lot of encouragement, why not do the same with them but on a different forum?'

I invited five friends and all responded, a great result! Two and a half months into writing devotions the Holy Spirit challenged me to produce a book using the devotionals we had already written as the base for it.

How does the book work?
Instead of producing one massive book that has over 400 pages, we wanted to create something a little more manageable and less costly to purchase. We have therefore created four books that contain three months' worth of material, one for every season.

Days one through five consist of devotionals.

The sixth day is a testimony day, an account written by a pastor's wife about her salvation or experience on the harvest field.

The seventh day is an empty double page spread entitled 'Study/Sermon Notes' to encourage you to write your own devotion, study a scripture you have read in the week, take notes on a sermon, or journal what God is speaking to you about.

Bible in a year/Bible in two years
This book includes a custom made 'Bible in a year' and 'Bible in two years' programme at the top of every page like this:

Y1 - Genesis 1 & 2 / Y2 - Matthew 2 & 3

'Y1' refers to the first year where you will be reading through approximately half of the bible. 'Y2' refers to the second year where you will complete it by reading the other half of the bible. Alternatively, you can read 'Y1 & Y2' at the same time and complete the bible in one year. You can also print the full bible plan in pdf format from our website at www.pwdevotion.co.uk

The struggle to maintain bible reading is universal. Sometimes you must go back to basics; picking up your bible on the odd occasion will not carry you through. Therefore, we have produced a simple plan that accommodates all lifestyles, a plan that can get you consistently reading God's Word (without being overwhelmed). A plan that requires discipline yet inspires achievement. The plan works through one book of the bible at a time, alternating between the Old and New Testaments.

Additionally, in the back of the first book you will find a list of (whittled down) recommended reading that covers a range of topics which have helped many pastor's wives over the years. We hope this helps you!

Who are the authors?
The authors (in all four volumes) consist of thirty-three wives of current pastors, evangelists and missionaries, as well as those who have served in this capacity in the past. This mix was thought important to get both a current dimension and to glean from the women who have returned home after their time on the harvest field as their wisdom and knowledge bring a special aspect of insight and depth to the book.

The nature of the book
I'm sure you have already gathered that we are not professional writers, but we are women with experience, spiritual revelation and a desire to serve. In my initial pitch to invite these women to join the project, I understood that some would find it a breeze, some a challenge and others an impossible task. I

stressed that their writing ability was not important (that's why we have editors) and it was in fact their insight and experience we desired.

Included in this book are devotionals and testimonies that are raw, insightful, unusual, deep, heart-breaking, witty, inspiring, uplifting, encouraging, and convicting, but I can assure you, all will leave you with hope and vision.

The purpose of this book
There are a handful of books written for the pastor's wife out there, but it seems, nothing quite like this. Over the years, having spoken to many pastors' wives, I have developed a growing concern regarding their personal relationship with God. You will invest in what you love.

Luke 10:27 (NIV)
He answered, 'Love the LORD your God with all your heart and with all your soul and with all your strength and with all your mind...'

For some pastors' wives it seems that their primary investments are elsewhere. Children, possessions and even the ministry, can consume you to the point that you lose a sense of urgency when it comes to having an intimate, active and a blossoming relationship with your Saviour. My prayer is that every pastor's wife, strong in the Lord or not, will dedicate themselves to seeking Him with all their soul, strength, and mind.

Here are a few objectives for the pastor's wife using this book
- Cause her to prioritise a devotional life of prayer, reading and studying the word of God; and as a result, change, grow, be restored, have fruit and be equipped for the good fight.
- Help her to understand and embrace the importance of her example.
- Inspiration for the harvest field.
- Clarity to this role she has been called to.
- Bring unity; we are all in this together.

'It's not always easy, but it's simple.'

This has become my motto in living my Christian life. I speak from experience when I say that I spent years trying to fight the 'duvet demon' to get up and pray in the morning. What I found is that fighting the flesh is not without effort, but it is a straightforward task. Fighting for the routine of praying and reading in the morning, coupled with studying the Word at a point during the week, has brought huge change in my life and I pray it will for you also.

Why pastors' wives?
Maintaining a consistent, close connection with God is a challenge for almost every Christian. It seems that once a couple of steps have been taken into the ministry, the devotional life can be one of the first things to be assaulted. The pressures build up, duties pile up, exhaustion sets in and before you know it,

instead of feeling victorious you are left thirsty and dried out. I want to declare to you that this does not have to be the norm.

The pastor's wife is the silent server. Like a backbone, her ability to function practically and spiritually affects her husband, children, church, the community around her and potentially the world. My prayer is that she can operate consistently whilst soaking in the joys of life and the wonderous blessing of the Cross.

The proceeds of the book
100% of the profit will be donated to world evangelism.

Charlotte Claxton x

FOREWORD

At the beginning of the COVID-19 lockdown, I was asked to be involved in a new lockdown challenge: produce a devotion inspired by daily reading and post it on the WhatsApp group on my allocated day. The purpose was to help each of us dig deeper into the word of God, develop a stronger prayer life, and maintain relationships during that difficult period. My initial reaction was, 'Me? Really? Gosh, I don't know if I'm able!' I felt inadequate, but nevertheless I enjoyed the challenge, so I agreed to participate.

If I can be transparently and painfully honest before lockdown my mind was in shatters and so was my relationship with God. I had fallen into a deep pit. I was questioning my worth, wrestling with condemnation, and feeling entirely useless. Starting to creep in were thoughts of self-hatred and punishing myself, of being undeserving of everything I had. It got to the point where I didn't feel worthy to hold my child. I felt disbelief in my husband's words of love for me as I could no longer love myself. I felt so alone. The shame of these thoughts were unbearable, knowing they were ungodly, and continually saying to myself, 'Pastors' wives shouldn't think like this.' I felt like I was sinking and there was nothing I could do about it.

Little did I know God was fighting for me and He was making a way out. The challenge of writing a devotion every week caused me to read the Bible like never before. I experienced how relatable, encouraging, and challenging it was, and the more I read and prayed, the more I knew God and hungered for Him. Right there was the beginning of my deliverance.

When I look back, it's bizarre to think that I genuinely couldn't work out the solution because I *always* fully believed that Jesus was *always* the answer. Since this change in my devotional life, I can see clearly again. It is becoming easier to rationalise and look forward. I am slowly but surely growing in wisdom and discernment, and instead of falling apart at the first hurdle, I am taking a step back and assessing the situation and thus bringing it before God. I've learnt that God's timing is perfect down to the very second. He peels back layers bit by bit and gives you the resources to deal with all aspects of life. He is all we need and all we can depend on.

Matthew 10:30-32 (NKJV)
But the very hairs of your head are all numbered. Do not fear; therefore, you are of more value than many sparrows.

I received this verse from a preacher within the first few months of my salvation. Now, possibly for the first time, I believed it. Why? Because I have started to know God for myself on a personal level.

This book is a tool to help you develop or renew your own devotional life and draw you into a deeper relationship with Him. There is a direct correlation between seeking God and deliverance. The joy I feel now is no coincidence. I have yet to master the discipline of a consistent devotional life, but now I have the revelation I need to keep fighting for it because of the dimension that has been added to my life by viewing God as a personal God, a literal father, and a sincere friend.

Anon

July 1st – *Testimony*

Y1 – Ps 52 / Y2 – Jer 6

Salvation Story by Linda

As a child of about nine, God was my invisible friend (although my parents thought otherwise). I would talk to Him every day and share my concerns, mostly about my fears. Dad was very dominating, with a short fuse and a violent temper, and he would often beat me, badly losing control. So, driven by fear, I lacked confidence in everything I did or attempted to do.

I was not allowed friends over to my house and the only time I got to socialise was at school or in the neighbourhood. I inherited my sister's bicycle and this meant I could go to see my friends (sometimes very far), but I also had a strict curfew with severe consequences if broken. One day I was late and I could see my dad waiting for me in the hallway. I knew what was coming, so I turned around and started running up the road, closely followed by my dad. I was so scared, my heart was thumping in my chest, but I just ran. I looked over my shoulder and realised he was falling behind. I shouted, 'Hey dad, I'm faster than you and you can't catch me!' He answered, 'You have to come home sometime!' The trick was not to return until he had calmed down. The beatings drove me to run away from home when I was thirteen, again at fifteen, and finally I left for good at sixteen years old.

I eventually moved cities and, little did I know, that would be where my salvation story began. I was walking in the city centre one day and I met a lovely lady who simply asked if she could give me an invitation to come to church. I took that invitation, hugged her, and promised to see her on the coming Sunday morning, which I did. This was a miracle in itself, because a week prior I had asked God to send me someone who would invite me to the church He had chosen for me. That Sunday the pastor preached on rejection and it was if God was speaking directly to me. I gave my life to Jesus that service and was baptised.

My dad didn't speak to me for years after I left, but since becoming a Christian, I worked hard to rebuild the relationship. After a few years my dad was rushed to hospital and was in a coma. I asked God to wake him so that I could tell him about Jesus and lead him to salvation. I slept in the hospital for a week, spending every day with him until God answered my prayer.

My dad awoke and, by the grace of God, accepted Jesus as his Lord and Saviour. He slipped into eternity in the early hours of that morning and I had the pleasure of holding his hand as he went. My dad and I were alone, but the room was filled with the Holy Spirit and we were both blessed.

God helped me to forgive, delivered me from fear, and has given me a peace in my heart. I married in the church and have been privileged to be a part of what God is doing in our fellowship.

If you have a family member who you struggle to believe can be saved, just remember we serve a mighty King who will give them the chance to get right with Him, even in their last breath.

July 2nd – *Jehovah Adonai*

Y1 – Deut 9 & 10 / Y2 – Is 29 & 30

Jeremiah 44:26 (KJV)
Therefore hear ye the word of the LORD, all Judah that dwell in the land of Egypt; Behold, I have sworn by my great name, saith the LORD, that my name shall no more be named in the mouth of any man of Judah in all the land of Egypt, saying, The Lord GOD liveth.

Although we see Yahweh pop up frequently (both Adonai and Yahweh means 'The Lord'), Adonai gives us more of a hint about the Lord's role in our lives. Adonai means 'master' or 'Lord,' showing God has sovereignty over us. In this verse, God is commanding that no man of the tribe of Judah dwelling in Egypt should use this title for God, because they were glorifying Him in word, yet profaning His name by worshipping idols.

When we call God 'Adonai' or 'My Lord' it shows the relationship of a servant to a sovereign master, indicative of supreme authority on the master's part. The word is used to show a level of submission where the servant has full dependence on the master. Understandably then God would be infuriated calling Him Adonai yet worshiping idols. We should all have a full dependence on God as Adonai. This is not in word only, but our life should evidence obedience to His direction and will as our master.

Isaiah 25:8 (KJV)
He will swallow up death in victory; and the Lord GOD will wipe away tears from off all faces; and the rebuke of his people shall he take away from off all the earth: for the LORD hath spoken it.

If Adonai is our Lord, He can give us direction, knowing there will be full obedience, supply all our needs with unrestricted access to His provision, and protect us with His power and might. We can also trust that no situation is unseen by Him, our tears will be wiped away, and no rebuke or shame will remain.

Lord, may I grow in the love for and knowledge of you. Let me honour you in every area of my life, that you truly will be Adonai to me. Amen.

July 3rd – *Your Flock*

Y1 – Deut 11 & 12 / Y2 – Is 31 & 32

Proverbs 27:23 (NLT)
Know the state of your flocks, and put your heart into caring for your herds.

God has given every pastoral couple their own flock to steward, each one different, but equally as special. No matter how quirky the sheep may be, the Bible directs us to put our heart into caring for His herd. He calls us to love them and give them the best part of us, reflecting Jesus and His love for souls.

Every pastor's wife will feel an element of responsibility for the flock. Our heart goes out to women, children, adolescents, homeless, and the fatherless as we long to see their lives transformed by the power of a living God. For the majority of pastor's wives, the flock that depends on us the most is our family.

Whilst this scripture can apply to the church, I have come to view my family as my God given flock. Seasons come and go, at times we see less of our family and other times where we see too much of them, but it is my responsibility to care for them, to know what is going on, what works well, where potential problems may arise, and ways to overcome this to function more effectively.

Who do you feel responsible for?

On our opening church service, I was willing, organised, and prepared to play keyboard. I was ready! However, when we began, I realised that I had overlooked one small detail: I had two children under the age of three! Where were they going to sit? And with whom? I'd forgotten to consider my flock and overlooked their needs. Needless to say, I took care of my flock and probably did the ears of the visitors a favour.

Knowing the state of *your* flock is essential for their equipping and ensuring the furtherance of the gospel in their lives. Love them, care for them, and attend their needs.

July 4th – *Made Pure*
Y1 – Deut 13 & 14 / Y2 – Is 33 & 34

1 John 1:7-9 (ESV)
But if we walk in the light, as he is in the light, we have fellowship with one another, and the blood of Jesus his Son cleanses us from all sin. If we say we have no sin, we deceive ourselves, and the truth is not in us. If we confess our sins, he is faithful and just to forgive us our sins and to cleanse us from all unrighteousness. (NKJV swaps cleanse for purify)

Webster's definition of cleansing is, 'Purifying; making clean; purging; removing foul or noxious matter from; freeing from guilt.'[1] This definition suggests to me that it is like a sickness, disease, or infection from which we need to be cleansed. Thank Jesus, we don't have to scour, pick, and scratch at the sickness of our sin. Jesus takes it *all* away when we pray for forgiveness.

Isaiah 1:18 (NLT)
"Come now, let's settle this," says the LORD. "Though your sins are like scarlet, I will make them as white as snow. Though they are red like crimson, I will make them as white as wool."

He purifies us! How simple! How humbling! We try to change to make ourselves clean, but with one prayer of repentance, it can all be just washed away. When you ask God to forgive you, He does! Believe it! He is willing to do so in order for you to be free.

2 Peter 3:9 (NIV)
The Lord is not slow in keeping his promise, as some understand slowness. Instead he is patient with you, not wanting anyone to perish, but everyone to come to repentance.

Lord, you're my loving Father and you're always there with open arms to cleanse me of my failures. Thank you Jesus for making it so simple that I can be made pure. I pray that when I feel conviction, I would come to you straight away for forgiveness and not wallow in condemnation. Amen

July 5th – *Stewarding Time*

Y1 – Deut 15 & 16 / Y2 – Is 35 & 36

Ephesians 5:16 (NKJV)
Redeeming the time, because the days are evil.

Something we are all very good at is wasting time, whether it's through procrastination or laziness, we've all been there! I was thinking about this topic and it occurred to me that people who have no sense of time are lost. Remember those blissful holidays when you've lost complete track of time and wonder, 'What day is it again?'

The word 'redeem' means to 'buy up'[1] or 'the payment of a price'[2] and seems to instruct us to view our time in a similar way to how we make money!

If this is the case, then here are a few things this could mean

- Budget time - to be organised and wise with how much time we are spending on certain things.
- Value time - put it towards worthwhile things.
- Track time - it's wise to know how much you have left. Just as it's a good thing to know how much money is in your bank account, it's a good idea to know how much time you have. When we manage time well, it is rewarding and positively affects everything around us.

There's a great old saying, 'If you want a job done, then ask a busy person.'[3] This seems counterintuitive, however, it's so true! Busy people usually know how to manage their time. The idea behind redeeming the time mentioned in the scripture is that you buy up opportunities, like a shrewd businesswoman and make the most of every opportunity for Jesus Christ.

Ephesians 5:16 (NLT)
Make the most of every opportunity in these evil days.

The wife of a minister spins many plates and managing your time will contribute massively to the effectiveness of your life. Prioritising, planning ahead, and allowing yourself time to regroup are all important elements of achievement. I should mention that self-care is also vital and often neglected! Developing a hobby, chatting with a friend, reading a book, spending time in the Word, or just relaxing are all valid time investments that will contribute to your personal feeling of accomplishment.

July 6th – *Friend in Need*
Y1 – Deut 17 & 18 / Y2 – Is 37 & 38

Proverbs 17:17 (NLT)
A friend is always loyal, and a brother is born to help in time of need.

Friendship is such an important part of our lives, and this is no different for a pastor's wife. A common piece of advice that was given to me before my husband and I went into the ministry was not to isolate myself and to reach out to my friends as much as I could (sometimes make new ones).

Of course, there have been seasons of busyness when I haven't spoken to my friends for a couple of days or even weeks. But in a time of loneliness (because let's be honest, pioneering a church can be lonely, right?!), all I needed was to talk to a sister on the phone and suddenly my mood completely shifted and I felt encouraged, restored and sometimes I received a well needed challenge!

Maybe you already feel you go out of your way to encourage people, call people and be a good friend. But the question is, *how much more of a friend can you be to people?* Whether it's a lady in your church, a friend you've had for years, or even your husband, friendship covers so many areas and is needed by all. Perhaps pray and ask the Holy Spirit to specifically lay someone on your heart that you could call or visit and just be a friend to.

John 15:15 tells us that Jesus calls us His friends. Now that should bring some comfort! Our friendships can grow and be nourished over time as we invest in them and it's so amazing that this is also true with our friendship with Jesus.

July 7th – *Testimony*

Y1 – Ps 53 / Y2 – Jer 7

Missed Opportunity by Hannah

It was a scorching hot day, I was sitting at the back of the bus on my way home from work, and opposite me was a lady with her son. Whilst choosing the next song on my playlist, God spoke to me, 'Tell this lady that I love her!' It was so out of the blue that I didn't really know how to react, so I just kept scrolling on my phone. When God speaks to me, I often feel a burden on my heart, and I felt it then, but I'm sorry to say, I did nothing. It felt like such an inconvenience and I honestly just didn't want to face rejection from someone who could potentially be sitting next to me for the rest of my journey. Boy did I regret that decision! The lady clicked the buzzer to let the driver know to stop and she got off the bus with her son. As she walked past my window I could see tears in her eyes; she had been crying and I didn't even realise. Of course, immediately I felt a pang in my chest and a lump in my throat because I had missed an opportunity for God to touch a soul. She needed to hear a word from heaven at that moment and God had wanted to use me to deliver it and perhaps lead her to Christ.

Since that day, I have prayed that when I am spoken to, God would give me the courage to evangelise. I realise that evangelism is not an option, but it's something that God has commanded us to do. Therefore, He can and will give us the boldness to do it!

There are souls to win, *will you step out when God asks?*

Matthew 9:37 (NLT)
He said to his disciples, "The harvest is great, but the workers are few."

July 8th – *Study & Sermon notes*

Y1 – Ps 54 / Y2 – Jer 8

July 9th – Proxy Offense
Y1 – Deut 19 & 20 / Y2 – Is 39 & 40

2 Samuel 13: 28 (NIV)
Absalom ordered his men, "Listen! When Amnon is in high spirits from drinking wine and I say to you, 'Strike Amnon down,' then kill him. Don't be afraid. Haven't I given you this order? Be strong and brave."

You are probably familiar with this story. Amnon and Absalom are half-brothers. Amnon's wicked and perverse obsession with his half-sister Tamer, Absalom's sister, lead to her Violation. While he comforted Tamar and encouraged her to keep her heart right, Absalom himself was rightly enraged. This rage led to a deep hatred and plot to kill Amnon for vengeance.

Unfortunately, offenses are a part of life, but Absalom personally took someone else's offense. Have you ever been in this situation? I have known dear people who themselves have been violated greatly and found deliverance and healing in our wonderful Saviour. The nature of this story is a painful one, but I believe it illustrates the point well. Our focus isn't the violation of Tamar but the reaction and ownership of Absalom.

How we cope and process an offense as a pastor's wife is critical. Do we bite back or do we work through it, confront carefully, and give our heart to God? What happened to Tamar is horrific. Absalom can justly share in his sister's pain, but he does not deserve the right to act on it.

When someone speaks against your husband or children, or even a friend, do you allow your emotions to flare uncontrollable and plan payback? Or do you equip them with the Word of God and words of encouragement, teaching them to keep their heart right or talking through how they obtain peace in this circumstance.

Many offences occur due to a misunderstanding. Be the woman of God who can set the record straight. You do not need to fight the battles of the offended, the battle is the Lords; instead you can be the spiritual voice of reason that brings liberty and forgiveness. Your example is paramount.

Letting go of an offence is a decision. It is one of life's greatest freedoms.

Colossians 3:13 (NIV)
Bear with one another and forgive one another if any of you has a grievance against someone. Forgive as the Lord forgives you.

July 10th – *Useful Jael*
Y1 – Deut 21 & 22 / Y2 – Is 41 & 42

Judges 5:24-27 (NKJV)
Most blessed among women is Jael, the wife of Heber the Kenite; blessed is she among women in tents. He asked for water, she gave milk; she brought out cream in a lordly bowl. She stretched her hand to the tent peg, her right hand to the workmen's hammer; she pounded Sisera, she pierced his head, she split and struck through his temple. At her feet he sank, he fell, he lay still; at her feet he sank, he fell; where he sank, there he fell dead.

The Bible recounts some interesting stories. Here it is recorded that what Jael did was good and that she is 'most blessed' because of it. I think some background on the story is important.

Israel had been oppressed for 20 years by Jabin king of Canaan, and Sisera the commander of his army. The prophetess Deborah summoned Barak and told him that God wanted him to go to war against them and promised victory. Barak refused unless she went with him. Deborah agreed, but told Barak this meant Sisera would be delivered into the hands of a woman. Sisera escaped the battle on foot and ran to hide in Jael's tent, whose family was an ally. Jael showed him kindness, lured him to sleep, and then killed him (Read the full story in Judges 4:1-23).

So what can we learn?

- God can give you the courage to do something unusual. Jael killed Sisera at God's direction, even though she would have found this request baffling and intimidating.
- Be in tune with God so He can direct you to do His divine purpose.
- Don't be an ally with those who purposefully try to harm the people of God.

Jael means useful.[1] She was a Canaanite and therefore not a Jew, but was able to discern evil and be used by God. *How about you?* Develop your relationship with God, tune into His voice, be courageous in what He asks of you, and enjoy the blessing of obedience.

July 11th – *Looking Beyond*
Y1 – Deut 23 & 24 / Y2 – Is 43 & 44

Psalm 116:5 (NIV)
The LORD is gracious and righteous; our God is full of compassion.

God showed compassion to us by sending Jesus to die in our place, forgiving us, and giving us the gift of eternal life.

Matthew 9:36 (NIV)
When he saw the crowds, he had compassion on them, because they were harassed and helpless, like sheep without a shepherd.

Jesus was often moved with compassion for the lost and demonstrated His love by miracles of healing and deliverance and pointing them to a relationship with the father.

Colossians 3:12 (NIV)
Therefore, as God's chosen people, holy and dearly loved, clothe yourselves with compassion, kindness, humility, gentleness and patience.

The definition of compassion is a feeling of deep sympathy and sorrow for another who is hurting, in pain, or has a misfortune, and is accompanied by a strong desire to help the suffering.[1] Some translations replace the word compassion with mercy, which is a broader term.[2] Compassion is more specific, not just pity for another, but seeing the need and reaching out to help.

1 Peter 3:8 (NKJV)
Finally, all of you be of one mind, having compassion for one another; love as brothers, be tender hearted, be courteous.

Having compassion for 'one another' includes our husbands, families, co-workers, members of the congregation, and others in our lives who need us to sympathise and empathise with the good and bad. We must be humble enough to look beyond ourselves and have consideration for what people may be going through.

What stirs compassion in you? Does compassion compel you to act?

As the wife of a minister, we often see people in their lowest moments, times of failure, and crisis. If we can have a listening ear, kind words, and helpful actions it can impact their lives greatly.

Lord, let me see people as You do, be moved by compassion as You are, and minister healing and encouragement through Your love and grace. Amen.

July 12th – *Made Rich*

Y1 – Deut 25 & 26 / Y2 – Is 45 & 46

2 Corinthians 8:9 (NKJV)
For you know the grace of our Lord Jesus Christ, that though He was rich, yet for your sakes He became poor, that you through His poverty might become rich.

Jesus, as the Lord of all creation, is rich in divine nature. He became poor (a man on earth) for your sake and, through salvation and the purchase price of His blood, you are made rich. You are rich in His grace, mercy, love, peace, and joy, all of which are priceless commodities in our world. You have the certainty of eternal life, the gift of the Holy Spirit, salvation, and an intimate relationship with God. These are true riches indeed!

In a physical sense you are also rich. For example, God has blessed me with my husband, children, family, and friends. I have a house to live in, food to eat, clothes to wear, and the means to buy more when I am in need.

Philippians 4:19 (NKJV)
And my God shall supply all your needs according to His riches in glory by Christ Jesus.

There have been many times for us when finances have been very tight, yet God always provides and we have enough. Miraculously enough.

Can you identify ways in your life that God has blessed and provided for you?

It's interesting to think that God has made us rich in His grace by giving himself sacrificially; and it's through His grace we can have compassion, serve, and give ourselves to make others rich. *How could you show God's riches to others so they become rich in themselves?* After all we are blessed so that we can be a blessing to others.

Lord, thank you for Your sacrifice, that through You I am made rich. Thank You for all your blessings in my life. I need you to refill me daily with Your riches so that I may bless others. Give me the opportunity and insight to do so. Amen.

July 13th – *Current Plan*

Y1 – Deut 27 / Y2 – Is 47 & 48

Ephesians 5:15-20 (NLT)
So be careful how you live. Don't live like fools, but like those who are wise. Make the most of every opportunity in these evil days. Don't act thoughtlessly, but understand what the Lord wants you to do. Don't be drunk with wine, because that will ruin your life. Instead, be filled with the Holy Spirit, singing psalms and hymns and spiritual songs among yourselves, and making music to the Lord in your hearts. And give thanks for everything to God the Father in the name of our Lord Jesus Christ.

Paul warns us not to make thoughtless decisions, but points us to the Holy Spirit. Speak out the Word of God, sing, and give thanks to Jesus. God's will allows for our human failings and, if we mess up, He is redemptive and will never write us off, we are the only ones that can do that.

My husband and I returned to our mother church for redirection after pioneering for many years. The devil made every attempt to destroy us spiritually and mentally, but we made a concerted effort to fight and keep our hearts right. We had given everything and we felt exhausted, but God still had a plan for us and we were determined to make the most of every opportunity.

Maybe you have come home, you are undoubtedly struggling, but God has not rendered you ineffective. You are seasoned and your experiences have instilled unique qualities in you that other members of the congregation do not possess. Whether you believe it or not, you *are* valued and looked up to.

Do you understand the will of God? Do you believe that He has current plans for you and your husband? Do not lose heart. You are His precious child.

Rather than instructing us to process the past, this text challenges us to think carefully, with wisdom, about where we will step now and in the future. He reminds us that the days in which we are living are evil and, therefore, we should take advantage of every opportunity.

Father, my husband and I are struggling to believe that you have a plan for our lives now and in the future. Forgive our doubt. Today we commit our lives to completing Your will. We relinquish control and put aside the past hurts, failures and trials. Help us once again. Fill us with your Holy Spirit and put a song in our hearts to glorify You. We give you thanks. Amen.

July 14th – *Testimony*
Y1 – Ps 55 / Y2 – Jer 9

China Child by Anon

Our youngest son was nine when we became missionaries to China. Prior to this we lived in a small, middle-class, pretty town in England. His life was idyllic! He loved his football team, his school, and his church. Everything was stable and lovely. He'd heard the conversations when we talked as a family about going overseas to obey the 'great commission' and, unbeknownst to us, told God, 'Not China!' It was tough for him to navigate, but he accepted it as God's will eventually. I honestly thought the older kids would find it hard and, as the youngest, he would adapt the easiest.

Well, he struggled big time for our first year and there was a real demonic element to it. Going from a town of population 60,000 to a huge city of seven million, to be stared at, touched, constantly harassed for photos because you're 'so cute', not understanding the language, not liking the food, and beginning to see Chinese faces almost as 'evil' coming at you all gave this kid a constant struggle with feelings of being overwhelmed and anxious. I was processing all this as an adult and finding it challenging enough, so how does a child cope?

Obviously, we prayed for him, protected him, and guided him as best we could, but there came a day as we were getting ready for church that he actually broke. He was just laughing hysterically. I took him into our bedroom and sat him down and told him, 'It's ok, let it out.' Oh my goodness, did he sob! He kept apologizing, but I said, 'Don't be sorry, it's ok, it's what you're feeling!.' The tears were streaming down my face as I could feel his pain, as mothers do. Already in my head, I was composing my email, 'Dear Pastor, sorry, but we have to come back, I can't break my child!'

Before we left the UK, a sister told me the Lord showed her that our kids would thrive and that I needed to trust Him. I stood on this as a word from God. So I said to my son, 'Honey, you've got to hear God for yourself. You are part of this plan and He's going to help you!' We prayed together, he felt better, and sure enough, a few days later he heard from God! His heart became settled and he began to adjust.

One of his teachers had seen loads of missionary kids come and go over the years, so I had shared the struggle with her at the time to ask for advice. A couple of years later, she commented that our son was one of the most well-adjusted children she'd seen make the transition into Chinese culture. Amazing!

And now? He shares the gospel with people in Chinese, loves the food, and told me recently, after being in a room with 'westerners' and Chinese, he gravitated to the Chinese and felt more at home with them. We can trust God with our kids to help them navigate tough times!

July 15th – *Study & Sermon Notes*

Y1 – Ps 56 / Y2 – Jer 10

July 16th – *Unlock Revival*

Y1 – Deut 28 & 29 / Y2 – Is 49 & 50

Philippians 1: 12-14 (NKJV)
But I want you to know, brethren, that the things which happened to me have actually turned out for the furtherance of the gospel, so that it has become evident to the whole palace guard, and to all the rest, that my chains are in Christ; and most of the brethren in the Lord, having become confident by my chains, are much more bold to speak the word without fear.

Paul chooses to look at the positive outcomes from what he is going through. When Paul proclaims that his 'chains are in Christ,' he is stating that in everything God has a sovereign plan and that all these devastating experiences, instead of destroying the gospel, have actually advanced it.

Could this apply to the COVID-19 pandemic? The struggle is real, but God is able to use even this for His purpose. I know of five people who got saved in the first week of our local lockdown. One of my fellow wives in the ministry told me that people have been readily responding to the gospel at every weekly outreach and many have been attending church. Many pioneer churches have been able to access new, permanent buildings, because businesses have vacated them now they've discovered how much money they can save having employees work from home. These are just a few examples.

John 4:35 (NKJV)
Do you not say, 'There are still four months and *then* comes the harvest?' Behold, I say to you, lift up your eyes and look at the fields, for they are already white for harvest!

Be assured that God is in control and, without fear, proclaim the name of Jesus boldly.

Philippians 2:10 (NKJV)
That at the name of Jesus every knee should bow, in heaven and on earth and under the earth

Father, I thank you for the security I have in salvation and I am contending for my city, my nation, and indeed the world. In the midst of lockdowns and difficulties, I pray you unlock revival. I am asking that you would move beyond the chains and struggles people are experiencing and use these to draw them to you. Help me to overcome fear and speak the Word boldly. I trust you and am excited for all that you are going to do. Amen.

July 17th – *If Only*

Y1 – Deut 30 & 31 / Y2 – Is 51 & 52

Galatians 6:5 (NLT)
For we are each responsible for our own conduct.

Have you ever said, 'If only my husband didn't (insert a habit or flaw), my life would be (insert word happier or easier), and I wouldn't react the way I do now?' You can replace 'husband' in this sentence with your children, people in your congregation, ministry issues, the slow traffic, or almost anything in life! 'I wouldn't blow up in anger if' or 'I wouldn't feel jealous or compare myself if' is just blaming someone else or the circumstances we are in for our behaviour, when in reality we choose how we react to life.

Proverbs 21:2 (NKJV)
Every way of a man is right in his own eyes, but the LORD weighs the hearts.

Rather than turning the blame on others, we should look inward. The circumstances we are in reveal who we really are, God can change us. He wants to refine us so we can get closer to Him in relationship, transform our character, and make us Christ-like.

What do you need to change in your character? How can you handle the situations better?

Of course, God could change the circumstances we find ourselves in, but He might be using them as part of the refining process. One thing is for sure, God will change us as we pray and seek His ways. And remember, He will never allow more than we can handle through His grace.

Romans 14:12 (NKJV)
So then each of us shall give account of himself to God.

Lord, forgive me for not taking responsibility for my actions and reactions. I know You put people around me and use circumstances to help me grow and change. I ask that You would change me, that I may become who You want me to be, and that I may accomplish all You have for me. Amen.

July 18th – *Knock-Out!*

Y1 – Deut 32 / Y2 – Is 53 & 54

Proverbs 24:16 (NIV)
For though the righteous fall seven times, they rise again, but the wicked stumble when calamity strikes

Getting up again after a physical battle can be exhausting. Round after round of being punched and knocked down, leaving you with bruised muscles, broken bones, missing or cracked teeth, and a host of other obvious wounds that can be hard to hide and recover from. This is also true of spiritual battles! Although not as obvious on the outside, the emotional injuries are just as real and painful.

In this text, Solomon does not suggest that godly people don't struggle when it comes to a battle, but he does say we are able to rise again, and again, and again. God will equip us with the strength to continue.

Isaiah 40:31 (NLT)
But those who trust in the Lord will find new strength. They will soar high on wings like eagles. They will run and not grow weary. They will walk and not faint.

Not only can a spiritual battle be tiring, but it can lead to so many other dangerous issues like self-loathing, doubt, despair, or condemnation. These can be as difficult as the battle itself when struggling in private. Yet again, God gives us the assurance that He goes before us and fights for us.

Deuteronomy 20:4 (NKJV)
For the Lord your God *is* He who goes with you, to fight for you against your enemies, to save you.

Lord, thank you that you are with me through every trial, and that You do not give up on me. Provide me with the strength to rise up and continue. Lord, I thank You for Your grace and Your unconditional love that picks me up and does not condemn me after a knockout. Please continue to strengthen and guide me so that I would soar high on wings like eagles, praising Your Holy name in all of its glory and splendour. Amen.

July 19th – *Destiny Embraced*

Y1 – Deut 33 & 34 / Y2 – Is 55 & 56

John 15:16 (MSG)
You didn't choose me, remember; I chose you, and put you in the world to bear fruit, fruit that won't spoil. As fruit bearers, whatever you ask the Father in relation to me, he gives you.

In this scripture, Jesus tells His disciples that they were chosen by Him. We must remember that the disciples were ordinary people like you and me. Some of them were ex-misfits. They knew themselves and were well aware of their past. I'm sure they didn't feel like their lives would amount to much!

But Jesus said they were *chosen* for His glory! The definition of chosen is 'selected as the best or most appropriate.'[1] *Do you believe that about yourself?* My pastor once said, "The best that we could do on our own, was the day before we got saved. Everything after that is God's doing."

You walk with Christ, not because you hold Him, but because He holds you. He has chosen you and called you to bear fruit and make a difference in people's lives by loving and serving. You have a purpose in this world that goes beyond your own thinking or imagination.

Being chosen should cause us to act, not because we have to earn what God has given, but in order to step into what God has already chosen for us: a destiny that, if embraced, will blow your mind.

Father, I am so grateful that before the foundations of the earth were laid You knew me and called me to serve You. I believe that everybody has been called to serve You, but many deny You. Use me to draw them to You and fulfil the purpose You have for me. Amen.

July 20th – *Historical Women*

Y1 – 2 Cor 1 & 2 / Y2 – Is 57 & 58

Katharina Luther (1499 - 1552)

Martin Luther was an Augustinian monk who wrote 95 arguments against the Roman Catholic church and nailed them to the Castle Church door in Wittenberg, an act that stood in history.

Martin was a firm believer who worked to rebuild the church's foundation of faith, focused on the Bible being the final authority for Christians, and challenged fundamental Catholic doctrine. It's thought that some of the pamphlets he wrote were smuggled into the covenant where Katharina von Bora had been living since the age of five. A few nuns smuggled a message out to Luther stating they wished to escape, and he arranged a night time rescue. On 7 April 1523, the women were smuggled out of Nimbschen by a merchant delivering herring. Once in Wittenberg, the nuns were married off to eligible bachelors, all except for an older nun and Katharina who was strong willed, outspoken, and refused to marry the bachelor picked by Luther. However, as the years went by she let it be known she would consider marrying him. He had never given thought to marrying due to the risk presented by his enemies and his belief that he would be a martyr. Yet, on the evening of 13 June 1525, Martin and Katharina married. Martin is said to have written of the event, 'I feel neither passionate love nor burning for my spouse, but I cherish her.'

As Martin's wife, Katharina was attacked through insults, gossip, and lies along with her husband, by those trying to discredit him. This did not prevent Katharina from being a helpmate to her husband. She built the home, ran a farm, arranged lodgings to generate income, and ran a business in the community. She was known to regularly engage in Luther's table talks, discussing the reformation with students and professors after dinner, unconventional for a woman of that time. Luther trusted her with the business and loved her deeply. On Martin's death, after 20 years of marriage and six children, Katharina stated, 'My sorrow is so deep that no words can express my heartbreak.'

They worked together until his passing. They stood side by side through the highs and the lows of life and ministry.

July 21st – *Testimony*
Y1 –Ps 57/ Y2 – Jer 11

It's Possible by Anon

Before we tied the knot, my husband and I agreed on all the 'important' matters in marriage like finances, ministry, our future, but not on buying a house. My incredible husband had it in his head that a mortgage was too permanent, too much of a burden, and not suitable for a man who felt called to preach. The Bible talks about selling all you own and following Jesus and this was exactly what we had in mind, however our strategies regarding this differed.

After a couple of months of marriage, I invited a mortgage adviser to come to our house and 'educate' my husband; cheeky, I know, but praise God it worked. He realised that home ownership was a practical move, and it wouldn't hinder us, but would actually give us more stability in life. We opened a savings account and focussed on saving some money for a down payment in a short space of time.

Unbeknownst to us, God was about to change our path. We were offered the opportunity to take over a church in a city a few hours away and we humbly, but excitedly, accepted the offer. It didn't bother me that we weren't homeowners yet, because I felt we were heading in the right direction. Little did I know, those savings were all going to disappear to meet needs and circumstances beyond our control. I started to fret and, like a lot of women do when desperate for something, I took matters into my own hands. I started to explore different ways to obtain a down payment for a house, but reality set in and I soon realised I was going to have to wait, save and spend wisely.

I had experienced financial hardships prior to getting married, but never desperation. When we entered the ministry, I remember asking God to show me what need is like, because I wanted to learn to depend on Him, (crazy I know but I really meant it). I knew that this would involve sacrifice, but I wanted to experience it, as indeed others had before me. In this I learnt that everything was a season and that the ability to wait, whilst against my nature, was an essential characteristic I needed to obtain.

Timothy 6:6-8 (NKJV)
Now godliness with contentment is great gain. For we brought nothing into this world, and it is certain we can carry nothing out. And having food and clothing, with these we shall be content.

One morning in prayer, I was asking God for a million pounds (you know how it goes), and suddenly It occurred to me, 'What if I never own a house?' My immediate answer was, 'God, I would still serve you, in the ministry!' I relinquished control and let God have His way.

We worked hard, got ourselves out of debt, gave liberally, picked up extra jobs, had two children, and continued to serve the congregation. God came first. Today I can testify that we are the proud owners of a house. The list of 'must haves' for my house was audacious, but I offered it up to God and He did not fail me. Other offers for the house we wanted were far higher than ours, but it was ours that was accepted.

Just as we want the best for our children, God wants that for us. Just as we make our children work for their pocket money to instil character and wisdom, so God also does for us. Do not give up hope, be wise with what you already have, and God will bring the increase!

July 22nd – *Study & Sermon Notes*

Y1 – Ps 58 / Y2 – Jer 12

July 23rd – *Our Protector*

Y1 – 2 Cor 3 & 4/ Y2 – Is 59 & 60

Your mind is a battlefield. The fiery darts of the enemy are intended to inflame your emotions and can be quite effective if given half a chance. A thought, a picture you've seen online, something you've heard in a song, or a word of gossip. Sometimes all it takes is a negative impression that takes root and grows into feelings of anger or angst, worthlessness, depression and, in extreme cases, suicide, which we see so prevalent in our society.

Psalm 3:3 (NIV)
But you, LORD, are a shield around me, my glory, the One who lifts my head high.

Psalm 9:9 (NIV)
The Lord is a stronghold for the oppressed, a stronghold in times of trouble.

The word declares God is our protector, our shield, and our stronghold. A stronghold is 'a well-fortified place or fortress.'[1] God doesn't send us into battle and leave us there to fight alone.

Philippians 4:6-7 (NIV)
Do not be anxious about anything, but in every situation, by prayer and petition, with thanksgiving, present your requests to God. And the peace of God, which transcends all understanding, will guard your hearts and your minds in Christ Jesus.

Psalm 34:17 (NIV)
The righteous cry out, and the LORD hears them; he delivers them from all their troubles.

We are to ask God to deliver us from trouble and protect our minds in every situation. Why do we ask God to protect us, be our stronghold, and give us peace, only to then cast aside the shield of faith, leave the fortress, and come out from under His protection? He has given us the tools, but we have to take steps to guard our minds.

Lord, forgive me for allowing the enemy's lies to take root in my mind and life. I pray that You would be my stronghold and shield, guard my heart and my mind, deliver me, and fill me with Your peace. Amen.

July 24th – *New Normal*

Y1 – 2 Cor 5 & 6 / Y2 – Is 61 & 62

Psalms 18:2 (NLT)
The Lord is my rock, my fortress, and my saviour; my God is my rock, in whom I find protection. He is my shield, the power that saves me, and my place of safety.

'Babe, I feel like God is calling me to Madagascar, how about it?' Yikes! Whether it's having babies, being launched into the mission field, or even our children being launched into the mission field, there seems to be so many changes in our lives as pastors' wives. When I look back at all the twists and turns I've gone through I think, 'Wow, that's actually a lot!' I'm sure you could say the same! It's exciting and wonderful how our lives and ministry are constantly morphing!

On the other hand, these changes can be overwhelming. When I had my first baby, I thought to myself, 'Nothing will be the same!' And so far it's true, of course! Establishing a new normal and letting God be the immovable constant is what is necessary in our ever changing lives. Fixing our eyes on Him because it's all for Him! This verse says, 'God is my rock, my place of safety.' He's not going anywhere and we can depend on Him as our firm foundation.

There's a quote I love 'If the foundation of faith is not embedded in our hearts, the power to endure will crumble.'[1] We need faith in Jesus, not just for our sake and that of our husbands, but also for our children. When they see us adjust to God's plan, demonstrating trust in Him even when we don't understand everything, it can inspire them to live their lives the same way. Take each day as it comes and God will help you.

July 25th – *Concrete Heart*

Y1 – 2 Cor 7 & 8 / Y2 – Is 63 & 64

Ezekiel 36:26 (ESV)
And I will give you a new heart, and a new spirit I will put within you. And I will remove the heart of stone from your flesh and give you a heart of flesh.

It's Monday, again! Monday is my 'major house chores day', so I put on my Marigolds, tie up my hair, and tune into BBC Radio 2. This day, I was fascinated to hear that the next guest on the radio show was Richard Dawkins, the devout atheist. 'Great,' I thought, 'today is going to get juicy.' It did! After his introduction, the host opened the telephone lines for members of the public to call in and speak to him.

Lo and behold, a lady from our church called in to challenge him about the existence of God. She told Dawkins of a miracle our church had witnessed. A broken leg was healed instantly and, what's more, we had the scans to prove it. He refused to believe her, accusing her of telling stories and suggested that he would be inclined to investigate this case as fraud. Regardless, she boldly told him, 'Just as a robber doesn't look for the police, an atheist will not look for God. Unless you taste and try God for yourself you are never going to know that He is real. You can walk onto a motorway and proclaim you don't believe in lorries, but it doesn't change the fact you will get run over!" She smashed it, to say the least. In closing, the host then asked Dawkins, 'Has she not convinced you?' Dawkins replied, 'No!'

Richard Dawkins is a perfect example of someone who has a concrete heart. The man was unmoved, unwilling to compromise, and unaccepting of this lady's valid point. Is it possible that bitterness has caused his heart to harden? *Can you identify with that?*

Whatever the cause of your hardened heart, I want to encourage you. The walls you've built up cannot preserve you. God can help you and give you a new heart. One that is tender, humble, bendable but not broken, and most importantly surrendered. Bring the state of your heart before Jesus in prayer. He will give you a new spirit, it's not easy but it is simple. Receive what He has for you, no holding back. Jesus is the master heart surgeon!

July 26th – *Brownie Blesser*

Y1 – 2 Cor 9 & 10 / Y2 – Is 65 & 66

Genesis 1:1 (NIV)
In the beginning God created the heavens and the earth.

Isn't God a genius! Where on earth (excuse the pun) do you start by creating a universe, people, creatures, and vegetation. I struggle just to make an apple pie!

Jesus is an inventor. The word 'invent' means to design and/or create something that has never been made before.[1] It's impossible for us to imagine the blueprint God drew up in heaven before He spoke us into existence. One thing is sure, He had an infinite and a fool proof plan.

Do you have plans? Do you struggle to accomplish them because of the limitations your life presents?

The Lord wasn't confined when creating this earth, but as you know, we are. You may feel restricted because you're lacking in finances, time and energy, or even because you are married and have children. I want to remind you that the Lord operates without boundaries. As His children, we are more than welcome to ask Him to equip us and provide resources that we cannot on our own.

It is very easy, when dwelling on the restrictions, to feel down cast and lack the vision necessary to accomplish what you desire. You may say to yourself, 'What's the point in planning when I know it isn't achievable?' Well, let me tell you, there's nothing (with God's help) a little innovation cannot accomplish.

I once visited a fellow pastor's wife who had been baking brownies. I asked her what the occasion was (I thought it was me!) 'You've got to get them to come one way or another.' At that time, she and her husband were desperately struggling to get people to visit and come back to their church. Instead of being discouraged, she prayed, strategized, and came up this yummy idea. Pastor's wives are some of the greatest innovators on the planet! Rather than allow restrictions to hinder your plans, seek God and invent a way to bring them to pass. Don't get overwhelmed, He is your helper and can make a way.

July 27th – *Unity Triangle*
Y1 – 2 Cor 11 & 12 / Y2 – 1 Pet 1 & 2

Hebrews 13:17 (MSG)
Be responsive to your pastoral leaders. Listen to their counsel. They are alert to the condition of your lives and work under the strict supervision of God. Contribute to the joy of their leadership, not its drudgery. Why would you want to make things harder for them?

As wives we often hear about being submitted to our husbands, but the Bible says in this verse that all of us should be submitted to Godly headship and ultimately to Christ Himself. Over the years, I've recognised the importance of my husband's relationship with our pastor. A good pastor may say some challenging things, but it's crucial to come under that authority regardless. We must encourage and pray over that relationship and know that the pastor's wisdom is priceless and can save us many hassles.

Sometimes a gentle encouragement to 'ask for Pastor's advice' is in order, or a well placed, 'Have you spoken to Pastor recently?' The Psalmist shows us that the anointing flows down from the beard of Aaron, which is an image of unity between the brethren.

Some husbands might find seeking advice and asking for help an impossible task for a variety of reasons, but let it be God who does the work in him. Our job is to contend for this very special relationship between him and his pastor and believe God to break down the walls of division that Satan so often has built up. Reassure him that his pastor 'is alert to the condition' of his life. When the opportunity arises, prioritise time with your pastor and his wife, prepare questions, and glean from the experiences they have had. In doing this you will contribute to the joy of their leadership and open up doors for them to speak into your lives and ministry.

Whatever your circumstance is regarding this matter, bring it before the Lord It might take time, but watch Him move in ways you never anticipated.

July 28th – *Testimony*

Y1 –Ps 59/ Y2 – Jer 13

Salvation Story by Hannah

My parents are Christians so throughout my life I knew about God, but I didn't feel like I needed 'saving' nor did I really understand what salvation meant for me. I went to church and elements of it I enjoyed like seeing everyone and singing songs. It was obvious that people in church were different from the people I knew outside of church.

I started to question God's existence in high school. I was badly bullied. I started to feel really anxious and I would often fake sickness to skip school. I remember at one point I even considered overdosing on tablets but those thoughts would soon leave, really because of fear of death as well as the love given from my family. I would then consider the mess I would leave behind if I ever made that decision.

I was anxious with little self-worth, but I was really good at hiding it. No one knew what was going on. I'd smile it away and 'find my inner peace' which, thinking back, was ridiculous because I had none. Throughout all of this I would still go to church with my family. I would watch other people's lives change yet still I felt like I didn't need Jesus.

We had a concert at church and a lady gave her testimony. It really spoke to me, she said Jesus took her anxiety and shame away and gave her a new life. I wanted that! An opportunity was given to become a Christian, I prayed that night for God to forgive me of my sin and I accepted Jesus as my Saviour. My life was never the same from that moment on. The bullying stopped because I no longer craved attention within their group. My worth was in Jesus.

July 29th – *Study & Sermon Notes*

Y1 – Ps 60 / Y2 – Jer 14

July 30th – *Jehovah Shalom*

Y1 – 2 Cor 13 / Y2 – 1 Pet 3

Judges 6:24 (NIV)
Then Gideon built an altar there to the Lord. He gave it the name, The Lord is Peace. It is still in Ophrah of the Abiezrites to this day.

Jehovah Shalom, which is translated 'The Lord of Peace,' is the name Gideon calls the altar, he built when an angel of the Lord appeared to him and reminded him that the Lord had been with Israel from the beginning and was not going to abandon them now.[1] They were living in constant terror because of attacks from their enemy the Midianites, who had risen in strength and were planning on overthrowing the children of Israel. The Lord of Peace revealed Himself through the angel and promised that He would continue to go before His children.

'Peace is the antithesis of fear. It provides perspective, encourages hope, builds confidence, inspires courage, and affirms trust in the power of God. In a world where people are increasingly overwhelmed by stress, conflict, depression, anxiety, and financial, emotional, and physical uncertainty, the presence of Jehovah Shalom provides a peace that passes all understanding.'[1]

Philippians 4:7 (NKJV)
Be anxious for nothing, but in everything by prayer and supplication, with thanksgiving, let your requests be made known to God. And the peace of God which surpasses understanding will guard your hearts and minds through Christ Jesus.

It's so easy to let our minds drift and believe in the lies of the enemy, but God does not want us to live in fear! *Have you had those moments where your mind is so frantic you can't even concentrate?* Jesus can calm the storms in our mind with one simple prayer. We can find refuge in Him and overcome any anxiety because He is The Lord of Peace. Ask Him to fill you with peace today and prepare you with peace for the future, so when challenges arise you can fully trust in the stillness of the Lord.

Psalms 46:10 (NKJV)
Be still, and know that I *am* God; I will be exalted among the nations, I will be exalted in the earth!

July 31st – *Greatest Gift*

Y1 – Josh 1 & 2 / Y2 – 1 Pet 4 & 5

1 Corinthians 13:1-7 (NIV)
If I speak in the tongues of men or of angels, but do not have love, I am only a resounding gong or a clanging cymbal. If I have the gift of prophecy and can fathom all mysteries and all knowledge, and if I have a faith that can move mountains, but do not have love, I am nothing. If I give all I possess to the poor and give over my body to hardship that I may boast, but do not have love, I gain nothing. Love is patient, love is kind. It does not envy, it does not boast, it is not proud. It does not dishonour others, it is not self-seeking, it is not easily angered, it keeps no record of wrongs. Love does not delight in evil but rejoices with the truth. It always protects, always trusts, always hopes, always perseveres.

Paul is helping us remember that gifts, talents, sacrifice and good works are nothing without love. Love goes beyond our emotions and actions to a place of self-denial. It's so easy to get caught up in 'the doing' what needs to be done that we forget love should be our motivation. The focus shouldn't be on our sacrifice or how busy we are because without love this profits no-one.

Read through what love is and what love is not, then consider how you carry yourself and relate to those around you.

We can be so easily distracted in doing activities in the name of service unto the lord, and we focus on the gifts that encompass love. We so easily forget that love is the most important factor and should be our driving force. It is not natural for all our actions to be motivated by the love of Jesus. We need Him to touch our lives.

2 Corinthians 5:14 (NKJV)
For the love of Christ compels us

Lord, please help me understand your love for me and what I mean to you. Thank you for your forgiveness, goodness and mercy to me. Please show me how you see others, so I may treat them with the love you have shown me. Amen.

August 1st – *Jehovah Jireh*
Y1 – Josh 3 & 4 / Y2 – Lam 1 & 2

Genesis 22:2 (NKJV)
Then He said, "Take now your son, your only son Isaac, whom you love, and go to the land of Moriah, and offer him there as a burnt offering on one of the mountains of which I shall tell you."

Abraham obeys God's instruction, prepares to sacrifice his son, acting in faith, and believing that God would perform a miracle. God stepped in and provided a ram, caught in a thicket, to be the sacrifice. This is where the name Jehovah Jireh is introduced.

Genesis 22:14 (NKJV)
And Abraham called the name of the place, The-LORD-Will-Provide; as it is said to this day, "In the Mount of the LORD it shall be provided."

The Hebrew word 'Jireh' is translated to the English word 'provide,' but also means 'to see to it'.[1] Our God sees where we are, knows our needs, and provides miraculously for us. We can trust God for financial and material needs, but also emotional, relational, and spiritual needs as well. This text is also a foreshadowing of God providing His son Jesus as a sacrifice for our sins, so that we might have eternal life.[2] God calls us to obey and have faith, so that He might provide for us, as Abraham did.[3]

Hebrews 11:17-19 (NIV)
By faith Abraham, when God tested him, offered Isaac as a sacrifice. He who had embraced the promises was about to sacrifice his one and only son, even though God had said to him, "It is through Isaac that your offspring will be reckoned." Abraham reasoned that God could even raise the dead, and so in a manner of speaking he did receive Isaac back from death.

Thank you Jehovah Jireh, that You not only provide for us materially, but You see and know all our needs and have the power to 'see to it' that these needs are met. Thank you for your provision of a Saviour, so that I can be washed clean and be transformed. Help me to trust in Your promise and not doubt Your goodness. Amen.

August 2nd – *Like Literally*

Y1 – Josh 5 & 6 / Y2 – Lam 3

2 Timothy 3:16-17 (NKJV)
All Scripture *is* given by inspiration of God, and *is* profitable for doctrine, for reproof, for correction, for instruction in righteousness, that the man of God may be complete, thoroughly equipped for every good work.

When we read the Bible, it's very easy to just skim over it and not soak anything in. There was a time when I didn't truly grasp the idea that reading the Bible should also involve some study. As Christians, we need to digest the Word and absorb what God has given us, otherwise it will make very little impact in our lives. Personal meditation on the Bible in daily devotions and listening to preaching are the two predominant ways in which we can hear from the Word of God. If one of these is neglected, it can be very difficult to stay on track.

James 1:22 (NIV)
Do not merely listen to the word, and so deceive yourselves. Do what it says.

When we hear scripture we have to take it as complete truth, otherwise we can fall into the habit of doubting parts of the Bible. 'All Scripture is inspired by God,' not just some of it, 'and is profitable.' If God stood in front of you and told you something, you would listen wholeheartedly, right? That's what we must do when we read God's Word! We have to soak up every verse and let it dwell within us. Why? Because it is our protection and guide.

Eph 6:17 (NIV)
Take the helmet of salvation and the sword of the Spirit, which is the word of God.

Lord, I pray that when I read Your Word, I would soak up every aspect. Help me to digest Scripture and lock it inside my heart and mind. I cast out all doubt and conflict within me. Help me to believe that Your Word is the complete truth, that I may use it as my sword to fight against the wiles of the enemy. Please reveal the truths in scripture to my life. Amen.

August 3rd – *The Comforter*

Y1 – Josh 7 & 8 / Y2 – Lam 4 & 5

2 Corinthians 1:3-4 (NLT)
All praise to God, the Father of our Lord Jesus Christ. God is our merciful Father and the source of all comfort. He comforts us in all our troubles so that we can comfort others. When they are troubled, we will be able to give them the same comfort God has given us.

There are many ways we can minister to the women in our congregation (being the pastor's wife can often be advantageous). I like to focus on being a source of comfort to both newly saved and older saints. When people think about comforting someone, they may think of the 'there, there' pat on the back approach. Actually, the word comfort in the Greek means exhortation, refreshment, and encouragement.[1] It's the picture of strengthening another to stand.

That's exactly what we can do! It might be as simple as a five minute chat on the phone with someone who has just lost her job, praying with her, and maybe giving a scripture to encourage her. As we know, the amazing thing about being able to minister comfort is that it isn't limited to the four walls of the church. Just like the Holy Spirit is a comforter, we are able to imitate this through our own lives. The scripture says, 'He comforts us in all our troubles so that we can comfort others.'

Is there a precious woman in your life who needs comforting? Reach out to her, let God use you to minister!

Father, You are my comforter, my strength and my shield. Help me to see what you see. Help me to be sensitive to Your direction. Amen.

August 4th – *Testimony*
Y1 – Ps 61 / Y2 – Jer 15

God Increases by Chantella

My husband and I assumed the pastorate of a church several years ago and we had over 95 people in the transition service. In the very next service there were only 30, and less than 20 in the next. After a few services, we were running with a core of about 15 people. The fringe consisted mainly of students who left to go back home once university had finished. After about 18 months, various issues caused the church to slowly dwindle even further.

My husband moved buildings to bring refreshing, he worked hard preaching and outreaching, and held concerts and film nights, but we only saw a handful of visitors over a year period. For many services, it was just our family in attendance and one faithful student who had stayed throughout. One night a visitor walked in and said, 'Is this it?' He stayed for the service, ate all my chocolate chip cookies, smiled, and never came back.

During this period, we hit several low points. My husband and I would often be discouraged after an outreach or service, and many times I wondered if it was my fault. I saw a friend's church have a breakthrough sparked by an individual who picked up an invitation from *the ground* in an area they hadn't even outreached in; that can only be God. I heard other testimonies of churches who grew exponentially and thought, 'How could this be when our strategies are exactly the same?'

I came to the realisation that it's not up to me or my husband's tireless efforts, but Jesus who will build His church. Of course, we need to be steadfast and keep doing what we know to do, but I had to learn to trust God and believe that He has a purpose and a plan. He is working in us, and no matter what happens, He is in control.

August 5th – *Study & Sermon Notes*

Y1 – Ps 62 / Y2 – Jer 16

August 6th – *Fruitful Fear*

Y1 – Josh 9 & 10 / Y2 – 2 Pet 1

Psalms 128:1-6 (MSG)
All you who fear GOD, how blessed you are! How happily you walk on His smooth straight road! You worked hard and deserve all you've got coming. Enjoy the blessing! Revel in the goodness! Your wife will bear children as a vine bears grapes, your household lush as a vineyard, the children around your table as fresh and promising as young olive shoots. Stand in awe of God's Yes. Oh, how he blesses the one who fears GOD! Enjoy the good life in Jerusalem every day of your life. And enjoy your grandchildren. Peace to Israel!

Those who fear God will live a fruitful life. Not a life of constant struggle and necessity, but of blessing and abundance. Note that the family is the central feature of this blessing, which is the ultimate aim of every Christian mother. God says that He will bless the family who fears him.

'Your wife shall be like a fruitful vine: The one who fears the Lord may be blessed with a large, happy home. The home is happy in its very heart, and the children flourish. As they gather (all around your table) there is a sense of community and happiness.'[1]

Oil and grapes were two important elements of ancient Israeli society. They were by no means necessities for survival, but they made life so much better. A happy marriage and flourishing children are much the same. What a blessing they bring when they burst through the door and descend upon the dining room table in a flurry of love and joy. Let us mothers 'revel in the goodness' and never take it for granted.

Psalms 112:1 (NIV)
Praise the Lord. Blessed are those who fear the Lord, who find great delight in his commands.

The next time you teach and guide your family in the fear of the Lord, think of the fruitfulness He has promised to bring to your home.

August 7th – *Chief Cornerstone*

Y1 – Josh 11 & 12 / Y2 – 2 Pet 2

Matthew 21:42-44 (NKJV)
Jesus said to them, "Have you never read in the Scriptures: 'The stone which the builders rejected Has become the chief cornerstone. This was the LORD's doing, and it is marvellous in our eyes?' "Therefore, I say to you, the kingdom of God will be taken from you and given to a nation bearing the fruits of it. And whoever falls on this stone will be broken; but on whomever it falls, it will grind him to powder."

The ministry has taught me many things, but brokenness, desperation and humility are a few characteristics I have become more familiar with while pioneering. I've had my ups and downs but this scripture has been a blessing to me and a reminder to always look to Jesus. We must turn to *Him* (not our husband, children, parents or friends), the Chief Cornerstone, because without Jesus our faith is in vain. I remind myself daily that our church is here today because God said it was so, and it is He who has put His people in place.

People always say that my husband is 'on fire' and has so much passion and desire for souls. When I first came into the ministry, I asked myself, 'Do I have the same fire? Can I be broken and desperate for souls as much as he is?' I started to pray for God to give me a stronger zeal and longing for souls in my heart. Jesus is answering this prayer and continues to stir my heart with compassion and an ache for the sinner and the saint.

Have you personally allowed yourself to be broken on Jesus the cornerstone? Are you desperate for God to move? Are you staying humble in all that God has done for your church?

Father, please remind me daily to fall on You as the Chief cornerstone in brokenness, desperation and humility. I love You, I trust You and I thank You for all You are doing in and through my life. Amen

August 8th – *Without Reason*

Y1 – Josh 13 & 14 / Y2 – 2 Pet 3

Luke 18:17 (NIV)
Truly I tell you, anyone who will not receive the kingdom of God like a little child will never enter it.

"Kids, it's time for dinner, can everyone come to the table please?" I hear the patter of little feet coming down the stairs. We gather at the table and as we begin to pray, my husband and I notice that our four-year-old son is making the sign of the cross with his hand. This is not a gesture we are accustomed to, so I said gently, "Son, genuflecting is not something we practice in our family as it is a Catholic tradition and we're Christians." To which he confidently replied, "Oh, I'm not a Christian!" With a smile on my face I inquired, "Oh, that's interesting, what are you then?" My son looked over his shoulders, leant forward and whispered, "I'm a ninja!" We all roared in laughter.

Michael W Smith sings an awesome song called Missing Person, and one of the lines says, 'There was a boy who had the faith to move a mountain, and like a child he would believe without a reason'.[1] In our text, Jesus is asking us to believe as a child. He understood that when we 'grow up' our reasoning changes because of what life hands us.

We must receive Christ 'as a little child, without prejudice, pride, ambition, and vanity.'[2] Satan is targeting your childlike faith. He wants you to think that logic and human reasoning is the only way to navigate situations, but we live by faith. We give in faith. We pray in faith. We evangelise in faith. We do all of these things without knowing the outcome because we trust that our Heavenly Father has a plan.

Hold fast to the childlike qualities of trust and humility, as these are the characteristics that will keep you close to Him.

August 9th – *Wickedness or Godliness*

Y1 – Josh 15 & 16 / Y2 – Ezek 1

Psalms 1:1-6 (NLT)
Oh, the joys of those who do not follow the advice of the wicked, or stand around with sinners, or join in with mockers. But they delight in the law of the Lord, meditating on it day and night. They are like trees planted along the riverbank, bearing fruit each season. Their leaves never wither, and they prosper in all they do. But not the wicked! They are like worthless chaff, scattered by the wind. They will be condemned at the time of judgment. Sinners will have no place among the godly. For the Lord watches over the path of the godly, but the path of the wicked leads to destruction.

This Psalm shows the progression of when men are living in sin. At first, they merely do as advised by the ungodly. But afterwards, they become used to evil, stand alongside sinners who wilfully violate God's commandments, and eventually become the perpetrators of ungodliness. This progression can be a slow fade.

Who do you currently spend time with and how do you behave when you are with them?

When we delight and meditate in the law of the Lord, the Psalm says, we will flourish and our lives are fruitful.

We can see more than ever that the prosperity of the world is fleeting! Worldly possessions offer no protection or help when stock markets crash overnight; there is political unrest, or world pandemics.

The godly have a promise that we can be 'like trees planted along the riverbank, bearing fruit in each season.' The Lord watches over us, and our 'leaves never wither' and we 'prosper in all' we do.

Stand on this promise in prayer today!

August 10th – *Embracing Earthquakes*

Y1 – Josh 17 & 18 / Y2 – Ezek 2

Psalms 46:1-2 (NLT)
God is our refuge and strength, always ready to help in times of trouble. So we will not fear when earthquakes come and the mountains crumble into the sea.

If you are lucky enough not to have experienced an earthquake first hand, you only have to watch a couple of YouTube clips to partially grasp the intensity. The ground shakes, things begin to fall, and panic sets in. You cling to the things you hold dearest, hoping and praying that you will come out of it unharmed. As we know, earthquakes are measured using a Richter scale, which calculates the severity of the tectonic plates shifting.[1] Whether it measures a 1 or a 10 on the Richter scale, the results can leave us feeling uncertain and anxious, as if nothing can be trusted.

Many times the circumstances around us are things we have no control over. We don't get to map and can't keep control of things exactly the way we want to, leaving us overwhelmed by the feeling that things around us are shifting. When those times of instability comes in our lives, it is so important to remember that we must hold on to the stability of Jesus.

Just like in the Parable of the Wise and Foolish Builders[2], we must choose to root ourselves in the promises of God and not waver when the storms come. Some storms just ruffle our feathers, but others can shake us to the core, causing us to fully rely on Christ and building us into stronger Christians.

As long as we build our foundation on the Rock, we can stand firm in the earthquakes and trust in Jesus during times of uncertainty.

Lord, help me to trust in Your promise that You are always ready to help in times of trouble. You are my refuge and my strength, shelter me from the mighty storms and earthquakes. Teach me to embrace these uncertainties and be rooted in Your solid and firm foundation. Amen.

August 11th – *Testimony*

Y1 – Ps 63 / Y2 – Jer 17

Understanding Beauty by Anon

Growing up, I was ordinary looking; a bit chubby, had acne, and wore second-hand clothing (Can you hear the violins?). I was raised in church, had a strong relationship with God, and I was happy, so didn't bother me too much. As I grew older, however, the magazines I read caused me to feel inadequate and abnormal (Thank God I wasn't allowed access to social media).

Deception is an age-old strategy of Satan. He loves nothing better than to plant seeds of discontentment through comparison and then watch how it causes insecurity and ultimately an identity crisis. I thought I wouldn't find love if I didn't first look lovely. I wore tight clothing, mascara, and false nails in my endeavour to be 'beautiful,' often putting my pursuit of a godly character in jeopardy.

But, praise Jesus, I married the man of my dreams and he always builds me up with affirming words. Early in our relationship, however, I wasn't so easy to convince. I knew he loved me and meant what he said, but the dislike I had for my body and appearance ran deep and there were times it caused contention.

The change in my self-perception began when we went into the ministry. The challenge of serving others and self-denial caused me to seek God more than ever, and through this I came to realise that life isn't about me. The Bible teaches us that we save our life by losing it[1], He increases as we decrease[2], and we must take up our cross and follow Him[3].

Of course, there is nothing wrong with wanting to look good, but God is concerned with our character. From the heart flow the issues of life[4] that determine our decisions and our destiny. We must look outwards, guard our hearts, serve Jesus by serving people, and make others see the beauty in themselves by helping them understand God's unwavering love for them. I have found this to be the meaning of true beauty!

August 12th – *Study & Sermon Notes*

Y1 – Ps 64 / Y2 – Jer 18

August 13th – *Righteous Oaks*

Y1 – Josh 19 & 20 / Y2 – Ezek 3

Isaiah 61:3 (NKJV)
To console those who mourn in Zion, to give them beauty for ashes, the oil of joy for mourning, the garment of praise for the spirit of heaviness; that they may be called trees of righteousness, the planting of the LORD, that He may be glorified.

Have you ever started your day without spending time with Jesus? We all have, of course, and I've learnt it can put my whole day under a cloud. A peacelessness can overshadow the day consuming my time, thoughts and energy. Worries about work, the house, the kids, schedules, my to-do list, menus, and other 'cares of this life'[1] tend to crowd God out of my day and put me in a low mood. Yes, we do have responsibilities, but God wants to exchange our worry and stress for His joy and peace, much like a currency exchange, and that means acknowledging Him in all we do.[2]

Isaiah 61:3 (MSG)
Messages of joy instead of news of doom, a praising heart instead of a languid spirit. Rename them "Oaks of Righteousness" planted by GOD to display his glory.

The Lord can take our problems, and heaviness, planting in us the seeds of joy and praise. He wants to lay hold of those inadequacies in us and make them a place of strength, like an acorn planted to His glory, so all will know the mighty oak is His doing. God wants us to be an expression of His character of love, forgiveness, and joy.

Lord Jesus, help me to radiate Your joy, that in my times of struggle and heaviness You may shine through, in all of Your glory. I pray others may see Your work within me, encouraging them to seek You for themselves. Thank You Lord for giving me Your beauty, joy, and praise in exchange for my shortcomings and failures. May You plant righteousness in me so I can be a strong and graceful woman of God. Amen.

August 14th – *Feed Me!*
Y1 – Josh 21 & 22 / Y2 – Ezek 4

There was a period of time that I lived in constant fear. One morning in prayer, God showed me the state in which my mind was operating, and suddenly I could smell the coffee again.

That same night, my husband preached a masterpiece in our mid-week service on the very topic of fear. At the conclusion of the service, he asked to pray for everyone who was bound by fear and I steadily made my way to the altar. He laid hands on each of us, and as his hand reached my head the Holy Spirit touched me and I was instantly delivered. I felt such a tangible releasing from this demonic oppression that had mentally disabled me for months, without any cognitive awareness on my part.

My point is not about fear or God's ability to deliver, but about receiving from your husband's ministry.

1 Thessalonians 2:13 (NKJV)
For this reason we also thank God without ceasing, because when you received the word of God which you heard from us, you welcomed it not as the word of men but as it is in truth, the word which also effectively works in you who believe.

When your husband stands behind the pulpit, he stands zealous, desperate, and prepared to see lives changed through the message the Lord has shown him. His heart beats for souls and yours is one of them.

When was the last time you concentrated on his sermon (without criticising)? Do you share his passion for the Word? Do you inspire him to proclaim Jesus?

For most ministers wives, our regular dose of preaching comes from the lips of our husbands. We must learn to receive the Word of God through the man God has called him to be, and not as the man who can't cook, doesn't always clean after himself, or puts off mowing the grass. I challenge you to bring a notepad to the next service and tune in with a heart ready to receive. God always has something to say to His children and that includes you!

August 15th – *Using Gifts*
Y1 – Josh 23 & 24 / Y2 – Ezek 5 & 6

As a young girl, a regular pastime of my friend and I was turning up the volume to any Abba song, singing our hearts out and dancing, whilst holding a hairbrush as a microphone (If you haven't tried it, I encourage you, it's super fun). I've been told that I can hold a tune, but some of my friends have wonderful voices and can really 'wow' people with their singing. I've always thought, 'Why would I get up and sing when there's no way I can compare with them?'

My heart has always longed to do something for God, but my self-doubt has held me back, always believing the age old lie of the devil that I am not good enough. When my husband and I began our ministry, there was a need for me to accompany him in singing, but my insecurities were all consuming. During the COVID-19 lockdown, he was asked to record a livestream concert and wanted me (well, strongly encouraged me) to sing alongside him. I did have the desire to help, and God challenged me to do it, so I stepped out, but not with a lot of confidence in my ability.

1 Peter 4:10 (NIV)
Each of you should use whatever gift you have received to serve others, as faithful stewards of God's grace in its various forms.

After this, during a fellowship, my husband showed a lady our livestream concert. She turned to me and quoted this scripture and it really convicted me. True, being the best singer or public speaker, is not what the kingdom of God is about.

A faithful steward of God's grace is one who will use their gift to serve God and others. I encourage you today to put your gift to use, that is why God gave it to you in the first place.

Lord, You have given me ideas and an excitement of things I can do for You. Please help me to step out and in trust and obedience. Let me be a faithful steward of Your grace in my life. Amen.

August 16th – *Work Heartily*

Y1 – Gal 1 & 2 / Y2 – Ezek 7 & 8

Have you ever had someone walk into your church and before you know it, the hairs on the inside of your nose stand to attention as an overwhelming smell fills the air?

My heart went out to our 'smelly lady' so I offered to take her regularly to and from church. I would prepare and coach my children not to make any comments, but as soon as we dropped her off I would choke everyone with air freshener and grumble loudly. One day, my two year old piped up mid-journey and said, "Mum, how come every time she leaves the car it smells so bad and why do you clean the seats when we get home?" I wanted the ground to swallow me whole. Yes, I was serving, but I wasn't happy about it, and it was clear for the Lord and my two year old to see.

Colossians 3:23 (ESV)
Whatever you do, work heartily, as for the Lord and not for men, knowing that from the Lord you will receive the inheritance as your reward. You are serving the Lord Christ.

Whatever we do, we should do it as if it's Him we are serving. Our labours bring us no glory or praise, are unappreciated, and go unseen. However, we are instructed to work sincerely, warmly, with our whole heart, for it is the Lord who sees and is aware of our sacrifice. If we were serving Jesus directly, we would consider it a great privilege and, because of His grace, mercy, and promise to bless us, working heartily would be very easy. The apostle Paul implores us to have this mindset in whatever we do and for whomever we are serving.

Today, serve others as though you were serving Jesus Himself. At the end of the day ask yourself, 'How has this change of perspective benefitted me and those whom I served?'

August 17th – *Historical Women*

Y1 – Gal 3 & 4 / Y2 – Ezek 9 & 10

Ruth Bell Graham (1920 – 2007)

Ruth was born on 10 June 1920, in Qingjiang, Jiangsu, Republic of China where her parents were medical missionaries. When she was 13, she was enrolled in The Pyongyang Korean School for Foreigners (North Korea) and that is where her love for Jesus really blossomed and her personal relationship with Christ began. Her heart's desire was to become a missionary just like her parents, but little did she know what God had in store for her after moving from North Korea to the US where she met and married Billy Graham.

After a brief stint as a suburban pastor, Billy became an evangelist for Youth for Christ. While her husband was away on extended national and international evangelistic crusades, she looked after their five children and often taught Sunday school in their local church. Ruth was a vital part of Billy Graham's evangelistic career and he often turned to her for advice and input about ministry decisions. Ruth often felt lonely without Billy by her side throughout the day, and she sometimes slept with one of his jackets to keep the smell of him close to her.[1]

Imagine the sacrifice of waving goodbye to your husband as he went off to preach somewhere, maybe for a couple of months, whilst you stayed at home with the children. Pretty tough! Even during the birth of their first daughter, Billy was away preaching! Ruth's daughter mentioned that she'd never heard her mother complain.[2]

Although her dream to be a missionary wasn't something she did, Ruth's relationship with God was strong, her love and compassion shone through, and she reached many people with her books, poetry, and her ministry in their church. She also released her husband to his ministry which resulted in thousands of people giving their lives to the Lord.

On 14 June 2007, Ruth Bell Graham went to be with the Lord at age 87. I'm sure she had her ups and downs as an evangelist's wife, but she lived an incredible, fulfilled, and blessed life, clinging onto Jesus until the end.

August 18th – Testimony

Y1 –Ps 65/ Y2 – Jer 19

Rejection & Redemption by Sophie

Beneath the normal looking home life people thought I had, my Dad was a violent alcoholic. He was always drunk or asleep and my mum was left to do everything for me and my brother. I would hardly see him and I had no real relationship with him, but I pretended that he was the best dad ever because I wanted to believe that he was. Feeling rejected by him, I looked to other things to get attention, constantly trying to fit in, be appreciated, or loved by someone.

As I got older, my brother developed psychosis and all family attention was on him. I didn't feel like I had anyone and I felt alone all the time. Eventually, I met an older boy in my school and I thought, 'Finally, I had someone who was interested in me.' Just before my 14th birthday, I lost my virginity. I liked the attention at first, but it quickly turned nasty and the bullying began. I had set myself up for humiliation and insecurity.
I was stuck in a vicious cycle, scared of losing his attention and the friends I'd made, but also humiliated by being used and his constant cheating. I finally decided to end the relationship because I knew I had to if I ever wanted to find peace.

Not long after, another boy was interested in me and again I became hooked on the attention. I slept with him, but hated it, knowing deep down this was not what I wanted. I remember praying whilst lying beside him, asking God to forgive me and get me out of the situation. Part of me thought this was the best I was going to get, so I had to take what was offered to me.

I just wanted to be loved by someone, but all my relationships felt forced or superficial. I think this all came from the same imaginative relationship I had with my Dad.

I came to church one evening and was so shocked at the fact that people complimented me with no hidden agenda. I instantly felt loved by these people around me and it was all because they were loved for who they were. God had opened my eyes. I had self-hatred for the things I'd done and didn't think anyone could forgive me, but through receiving God's forgiveness, I was set free from all my rejection and learned to forgive myself.

Knowing that God loves me and has forgiven me gives me such peace in my mind. His love is everlasting and He is the only one who can ever truly fulfil me. God doesn't reject me and has become the father I always longed for growing up. I was gripped by the need to be loved, but never found that outside of Christ.

Romans 8:31 (NKJV)
What then shall we say to these things? If God *is* for us, who *can be* against us?

August 19th – *Study & Sermon Notes*

Y1 – Ps 66 / Y2 – Jer 20

August 20th – *Michal's Response*

Y1 – Gal 5 & 6 / Y2 – Ezek 11 & 12

2 Samuel 6:16 (NKJV)
Now as the ark of the Lord came into the City of David, Michal, Saul's daughter, looked through a window and saw King David leaping and whirling before the Lord; and she despised him in her heart.

2 Samuel 6:20 (NKJV) Michal to David:
"How glorious was the king of Israel today, uncovering himself today in the eyes of the maids of his servants, as one of the base fellows shamelessly uncovers himself!"

2 Samuel 6:22 (NKJV) David's response:
"And I will be even more undignified than this, and will be humble in my own sight. But as for the maidservants of whom you have spoken, by them I will be held in honour."

The word 'despise' means to regard with contempt and scorn.[1] Michal looked with scorn on her husband and despised his worshipping of God. The Amplified version includes, 'because she thought him undignified.' Her heart was pious and full of pride. 'Piety' is defined as devout fulfilment of religious obligations.[2] Michal was more concerned about what people thought of her husband, than she was with what God thought.

David tells Michal that he will be held in honour for the way he is worshipping. 'Those that honour God, he will honour; but those that despise him, and his servants and service, shall be lightly esteemed.'[3] God knows and sees the heart and it is not for us to despise or scorn. The Lord Himself judged Michal's attitude.

Do you ever do this without even realising? What are your thoughts towards your husband or others humbling themselves before God, going to the altar to pray when it was a potentially embarrassing subject, or even worshipping wholeheartedly?

Lord, help me to always be humble before You, have a heavenly perspective towards devotion, and not be concerned with outward appearances. Amen.

August 21st – *Not Robots*

Y1 – Jud 1 & 2 / Y2 – Ezek 13 & 14

Jude 1:22-23 (NLT)
And you must show mercy to those whose faith is wavering. Rescue others by snatching them from the flames of judgment. Show mercy to still others, but do so with great caution, hating the sins that contaminate their lives.

When I had my baby, to my questions (I had lots), my midwives would remind me that babies are 'not robots' and there is no 'one size fits all' approach. This caused me to think about the people in our churches, how they are all very different, and some ways of ministering might not be as effective for one as it would for another.

The same goes for evangelising. For example, a single mum traumatised by a past abusive relationship may be more open to the loving approach. She may be more receptive to the fact that God loves her and can heal her emotional wounds, rather than condemning her to hell if she doesn't repent! However, a rebel or a mocker might need the 'eternal fire' approach, 'snatching them from the flames of judgement'.[1]

Give time to learning the essential quality of people skills. Allow yourself time to take a back seat, observe people, be objective, and don't jump to conclusions. We should really learn to relax and enjoy people, showing compassion to the unrepentant sinner and those who doubt God, without condoning sin. If you find your mind reverting to the cynical, check your heart and be careful not to paint everyone with the same brush. Have faith that people can and do change.

1 Corinthians 9:22 (NLT)
When I am with those who are weak, I share their weakness, for I want to bring the weak to Christ. Yes, I try to find common ground with everyone, doing everything I can to save some.

Father, please give me the ability and skill to navigate people, to have a genuine heart of compassion, and to show Your mercy always. Amen.

August 22ⁿᵈ – *Immense Influence*
Y1 – Jud 3 & 4 / Y2 – Ezek 15 & 16

Daniel 5:29 (NIV)
Then at Belshazzar's command, Daniel was clothed in purple, a gold chain was placed around his neck, and he was proclaimed the third highest ruler in the kingdom.

Daniel had the most incredible influence over kings and kingdoms. This is no wonder, as he was a man who was unwavering in his faith and, regardless of the consequence, was a faithful, obedient, and gifted man who was available to be used by God.

Daniel found himself in a rather sticky situation regarding a den full of hungry lions.[1] Some envious officials plotted against Daniel by devising a law they knew he was already breaking. However, God's plan is always perfect. They had the power to feed him to the lions, but God had the power to shut the lions' mouths. Daniel lived because God used an obedient and willing soul who desired more of Him.

Daniel 6:26 (NKJV)
I (King Darius) make a decree that in every dominion of my kingdom men must tremble and fear before the God of Daniel.

Amazingly, Daniel became the third highest ranking ruler in the kingdom. His influence caused the king to demand that Daniel's God was respected and worshipped.

As a Christian, how do you affect the character, growth, and the behaviour of the people around you?

Lord Jesus, help me to emulate the character of Daniel. Convict me when I am disobedient and unwilling to do Your will above mine. Right now, I make myself available and I ask You to use me, as You did Daniel, to influence the people around me, impacting nations, and give me the character to maintain a strong faith and love for you. Amen.

August 23rd – *Cooking Ability*

Y1 – Jud 5 & 6 / Y2 – Ezek 17 & 18

Proverbs 31:14-15 (KJV)
She is like the merchants' ships; she bringeth her food from afar. She riseth also while it is yet night, and giveth meat to her household, and a portion to her maidens.

You've heard the saying, 'The way to a man's heart is through his stomach!' I'm not sure if it's 100% true, but food definitely meets a basic physical need of humans, which is crucial sometimes before they can get the revelation of having their spiritual needs met.

My mum was a single parent who worked full time and never cooked. We would eat microwave meals, cold food, noodles, or soup, which I actually thought was real food and a normal diet. When I got married, I only knew how to cook three or so meals. I had to change my mindset to actually plan and cook a homemade nutritional dinner each day and this was surprisingly difficult for me as it was an entirely new experience.

As pastor's wives, we reach out to individuals from the very initial stages of knowing God, to established Christians experiencing the ebb and flow of life. One way of encouraging people to open up and relax, is with good food.

Early in marriage, I was too embarrassed to invite a married couple for dinner, and actually didn't for years. I thought 'she bringeth her food from afar' meant a take away. But, in time, as I cooked for my household, I learnt the skill of planning successful meals with the finances available. Although many youth and single men were subject to culinary disasters, thankfully, I improved. Now I can prepare food not just for my household, but for visiting impact teams, unexpected visitors after church, and couples.

I laugh when people say my food is good because God reminds me where I started. Cooking for people has become a blessing. Many conversations have taken place over a good meal, which has supported individuals to reach their calling and strengthened them in God.

August 24th – *No Division*

Y1 – Jud 7 & 8 / Y2 – Ezek 19 & 20

Have you ever thought about the story of the Tower of Babel? What is fascinating to me is that God acknowledges when people work together in unity, 'nothing that they propose to do will be withheld from them.' Division is also powerful! When their language was confused so that they could no longer communicate, 'they stopped building.'

1 Corinthians 1:10 (NKJV)
Now I plead with you, brethren, by the name of our Lord Jesus Christ, that you all speak the same thing, and that there be no divisions among you, but that you be perfectly joined together in the same mind and in the same judgment.

The strategy of the enemy is always to divide, so we stop building and growing. This is true in marriage, a church, and even a fellowship of churches. Being part of a church planting ministry means we will have different 'mother churches' and 'family trees' so to speak, but we are all connected to the same vine. Although there will be variations in methods, different personalities, and creativity, we should always strive to have the 'same mind' or vision, the 'same judgments or convictions, and to 'speak the same thing' so there is no division.

1 Corinthians 1:12-13 (NKJV)
Now I say this, that each of you says, "I am of Paul," or "I am of Apollos," or "I am of Cephas," or "I am of Christ." Is Christ divided? Was Paul crucified for you? Or were you baptized in the name of Paul?

Ultimately, we are all followers of Jesus. The Bible is our standard for ministry, the pattern we follow, and the unwavering goalpost for life. There will be winds of false doctrine, dissension in the ranks, and even rebellion, but we must keep our eyes on Jesus and put Him first.

One thing I have learnt as a pastor's wife is that my personal convictions, vision, and doctrine must be firmly planted in His Word if I'm to stay the course and not be side tracked by things that divide us. Stay connected.

August 25th – *Testimony*

Y1 – Ps 67 / Y2 – Jer 21

Salvation Story by Patricia

I always ask my kids, 'What are you thankful for?' They both usually respond, 'I'm thankful for mummy and daddy,' but the other day one of them said, 'I'm thankful for God!' It melted my heart! Without God, where and who would we really be?

I gave my life to Jesus when I was 15 years old. I was going through a dark time in my life, dealing with rejection, emptiness, and feeling deeply unloved. My cousin and I had started looking for a church to go to because we wanted to make our grandma happy (Keeping up the family tradition was important to her). Admittedly, I had no plan to stop raving, drinking, and the occasional smoking. Then my cousin was invited by some folks on the streets of Hackney, London to a drama production called Heaven's Gates, Hell's Flames. She gave her life to Christ and was powerfully changed. I was bemused. I kept arguing that 'giving up our immoral lifestyle wasn't the plan' and 'who would get into mischief with me now,' but she didn't look back and continued being a great witness to me and our friends.

It didn't take me long before I went to church with her and gave my life to Jesus as well! I finally found the missing piece I was looking for and it's the best decision I ever made! He's a Father to the fatherless and nothing can separate us from His unconditional love! I am changed, changing, and truly blessed. Where would I be if not for Christ? I'm so thankful for my church, my family, my husband, my children, my friends, and for the opportunity I currently have as a missionary in the great country of China. I'm so thankful for everyone who has been patient with me, loved me through ups and downs, and showed me how to be a Christian, wife, mother, and friend. Most importantly, I'm thankful to Jesus, my God and Saviour, the one who took that broken 15-year-old girl and healed her.

Psalm 9:1 (NIV)
I will give thanks to you, Lord, with all my heart; I will tell of all your wonderful deeds.

August 26th – *Study & Sermon Notes*

Y1 – Ps 68 / Y2 – Jer 22

August 27th – *Little Moments*

Y1 – Jud 9 / Y2 – Ezek 21 & 22

Psalm 118:24 (NKJV)
This is the day the Lord has made; We will rejoice and be glad in it.

I don't know about you, but life doesn't seem to pause or slow down! This can pose all kinds of dilemmas, one of them is that we overlook the little moments that can bring such joy and beauty to life. You know the ones; they put a smile on your face and instantly bring a lift. We must take care to be in the present, choose to acknowledge them as gifts, and rejoice.

One Sunday morning had been especially difficult for my husband and I, with the usual chaos to get out of the door on time, keeping the children relatively clean, whilst at the same time stopping them from killing each other. We got to church and started going through the routine of setting up for service as the children played and entertained themselves. Even though we were in a rush, my husband spontaneously started playing a nursery rhyme on the guitar and my toddler jumped in with vocals. She was so proud of herself as she sang and performed. She even shared the microphone with her younger sibling, a miracle in itself, and they were so cute. It was such a lovely moment and brought such joy to my heart.

Don't let life bog you down! Take time to notice the little pleasures; your husband bringing you a cup of tea, a snuggle with your children, a family walk, a fun fellowship. Pick out the positives and choose to be thankful. To see the glass *is* half full and not half empty. Rejoice in the day the Lord has made!

Proverbs 17:22 (MSG)
A cheerful disposition is good for your health; gloom and doom leave you bone-tired.

Lord Jesus, help me to have a heart that is joyful and rejoices in the wonder of it all. Help me pick out and remember the lovely moments during my day. Amen.

August 28th - *Spiritual Assaults*
Y1 – Jud 10 & 11 / Y2 – Ezek 23 & 24

1 Peter 5:8-9 (KJV)
Be sober, be vigilant; because your adversary the devil, as a roaring lion, walketh about, seeking whom he may devour: Whom resist steadfast in the faith, knowing that the same afflictions are accomplished in your brethren that are in the world.

1 Peter 5:8-9 (MSG)
Keep a cool head. Stay alert. The Devil is poised to pounce, and would like nothing better than to catch you napping. Keep your guard up. You're not the only ones plunged into these hard times. It's the same with Christians all over the world. So keep a firm grip on the faith.

You have an enemy! He seeks an opportunity to devour you like a lion would its prey! This is strong language. Sin seems like such normal behaviour in our world that it's easy to feel a false sense of security, but the Bible warns us clearly to stay alert and resist harmful temptations.

The devil is your adversary, a slanderous false accuser. When you have car troubles, job difficulties, marital tensions, health problems, or financial constraints, he is poised to pounce with anger, division, doubt, fear, or hopelessness. When these times come you need to be sober' maintain sound judgment and self-control, keep a cool head, and don't be caught napping. Don't forget who it is you are up against.

How do you keep your guard up and resist steadfast in the faith? We have the spiritual weapons of prayer,[1] the Word of God, and faith.[2] Know also, it is the same with Christians all over the world and you are not alone. Fellowship with other believers is so crucial. Satan will attempt to derail you, but the more you resist, the more authority you establish and the more ground you take. In the same way we hold onto the safety bars of a roller coaster, so should we keep a firm grip on the faith.

Lord You commanded us to resist the devil and You promised he would flee from us. I take dominion (name the issues) in your name and by the blood of the lamb.

August 29th – *Chain Reaction*

Y1 – Jud 12 & 13 / Y2 – Ezek 25 & 26

John 4:28-30 (NIV)
Then, leaving her water jar, the woman went back to the town and said to the people, "Come, see a man who told me everything I ever did. Could this be the Messiah?" They came out of the town and made their way toward him.

Jesus went against all cultural barriers and spoke to this Samaritan woman who was shunned by society and to whom most people wouldn't speak. He disregarded social obstacles and reached out to this woman in need, to share His message of love with her. The woman became a witness of the father's love and grace to the very people who mocked and ridiculed her, and many became believers through her testimony.

Does the outcast have a place in your heart?

Let no prejudice, bias, or social norm deter you from sharing the love of Christ. Kingdom culture trumps every other culture. The Great Commission[1] teaches us to include the Samaritan woman and be an ambassador to all nations for the gospel of salvation through Jesus. Only God knows the people they in turn could impact through our intervention. Make it a priority to speak to someone this week and share with them the love of Christ.

Lord Jesus, thank You for saving me! Help me to see past any barrier, prejudice, or bias to see the person and their needs. Give me courage and boldness to declare Your name in any way I can. May I be a light in the darkness of this world, leading souls to Your precious salvation and encouraging others to go and do likewise.

August 30th – *Free Will*
Y1 – Jud 14 & 15 / Y2 – Ezek 27 & 28

Gen 2:16-17 (NIV)
And the LORD God commanded the man, "You are free to eat from any tree in the garden; but you must not eat from the tree of the knowledge of good and evil, for when you eat from it you will certainly die.

One of the most common questions asked by non-believers is, 'Why is there so much evil in the world?' It's a very deep question, but one that can be answered with the simple response, free will! When Adam and Eve resided in the grand garden of Eden, the Lord instructed them not to touch the tree of the knowledge of good and evil because they had free will. He did not create clones who obey every command, He created humans with a heart and a conscience who knows right from wrong.

So why did God give us free will? If you bear in mind that our ultimate purpose is for a relationship with our Creator, you will understand that love is a choice. Love by force is not love at all, because love in its nature decides who and what it wants to embrace.

I received the revelation as a child that Jesus died for me. He hung on a cross, and sacrificed everything because of His love for me. I couldn't comprehend why people *wouldn't* choose to align their will to His. I made a choice that nothing would separate me from God's will and this has guided my decisions for years.

Growing up, I dreamed of starring on Broadway or the West End, which obviously never happened. However, God gave me a talent to be used for His glory and thus has always made a way for me to express it through our church productions and used for the purpose of winning souls. If that's not a win-win situation, I don't know what is. God Himself only knows, if I had pursued my will above His, I might not be serving Him now. That is not to say we can never follow our dream, only that we should always choose His will above our own.

Father, these are my dreams (name them). Right now I surrender them to you. I want to fulfil Your will for my life. Although I do not know what lies ahead I will trust you and wholeheartedly devote myself to You. I relinquish control and ask you to give me wisdom and clarity to discern Your will from mine. Amen.

August 31st – *Beautiful Feet*
Y1 – Jud 16 & 17 / Y2 – Ezek 29 & 30

Romans 10: 15 (NIV)
How beautiful are the feet of those who bring good news!

God used this scripture at a pivotal point in my life. It was a Friday morning of the Bible conference in which we were going to be launched into the ministry. I began to panic, 'Did God really want this?' I played Bible roulette and it fell open to this verse. God confirmed I had beautiful feet.

'Don't let your feet grow old and crusty!' Good advice! I heard this in a sermon by Pastor Wayman Mitchell when he was 90 years old. He said, 'This is a spirit, like that spirit behind soldiers in WWII, a spirit we must never lose in our work for God. To venture forth, to lay hold of God, and to see our mission accomplished.' We must march forward without distraction, relaxing, or turning back.

2 Timothy 2:4 (NLT)
Soldiers don't get tied up in the affairs of civilian life, for then they cannot please the officer who enlisted them.

Joshua 1:3 (NKJV)
Every place that the sole of your foot will tread upon I have given you, as I said to Moses.

Ephesians 6:15 (NIV)
And with your feet fitted with the readiness that comes from the gospel of peace.

How do we keep our feet moisturised and healthy?

I think this comes down to our personal convictions. This can be described as 'a special set of our beliefs that determine what you believe to be right and wrong. They drive your behaviours and actions in every decision involving right and wrong. They determine your response to other people's actions, including both your actions and your emotional response'.[1] When we lack convictions we ponder at every crossroad what to do, and never have a confidence about our decisions.

Plant your feet in the firm foundation of God. Keep following God's GPS. He will direct your paths and make your ways straight[2] for your beautiful feet.

Time to purchase your next Devotional book
Volume 4
October - November - December

September 1st – *Testimony*

Y1 – Ps 69 / Y2 – Jer 23

PKS By Heather

Isaiah 54:17 (NIV)
No weapon forged against you will prevail, and you will refute every tongue that accuses you. This is the heritage of the servants of the Lord, and this is their vindication from me.

It seems that the pastor's kids have a special target on their back. I think the devil specifically wants to sabotage our kids because we have chosen to accept our calling to the ministry. I know personally, when my children struggle it consumes me. Right or wrong, that's what happens. It causes paralysis and gives me tunnel vision. What better way to side-track us from our mission?

I've contemplated this, prayed about it, and observed these dynamics for 35 years. I took an informal survey amongst my own four children and some pastor's kids, both male and female, whom I know well. I asked, in their view, what were the pros and cons of being the child of a pastor? I found that they all felt the biggest negative was a higher degree of accountability, scrutiny, and expectation. They also acknowledged the positives were growing up in a godly home where they saw Christ's love played out daily and the benefits of having close contact with godly leaders, pastors, and evangelists. The lesson that I have learnt was that a spiritual dynamic is at work, for and against them. How else could a random group of pastor's kids come up with the same basic list?

Our kids are linked to our calling and we must be aware of the impact it has on them. First of all, we need to remind them that they are sinners who are in need of a saviour and of the grace of God. In addition, it is vital to communicate with them and show compassion. Acknowledge their grievances and point them to Jesus, the greatest problem solver of all. Prioritise their spiritual milestones, show attentiveness and excitement as you would towards a new convert. I believe if we do these things, we can give them an advantage in the struggles inherent in being a pastor's kid.

September 2nd - *Study & Sermon Notes*

Y1 – Ps 70 / Y2 – Jer 24

September 3rd – *Jehovah Tsidkenu*

Y1 – Jud 18 & 19 / Y2 – Ezek 31 & 32

Jeremiah 23:6 (NLT)
And this will be his name: 'The Lord Is Our Righteousness.' In that day Judah will be saved, and Israel will live in safety.

Jehovah-tsidkenu. What in the world do these words mean? We may know *Jehovah* is the personal name of God, which is translated as 'LORD.' *Tsidkenu*, less familiar, means 'our righteousness.' Altogether, *Jehovah-tsidkenu* means 'the LORD our righteousness' in Hebrew.[1]

So what does this mean for us? Righteousness is something *positive*. The work of Jesus in His people is not only to wash us from the stain of sin, but that the perfect obedience and righteousness of Jesus is *ours* in Him (2 Corinthians 5:21). It's encouraging to think that the righteousness that God possesses is what has been given to us when we turned to Christ. God has provided Christ, the Righteous One, and He alone satisfies God's demand of righteousness. It is a central characteristic of God's nature!

My husband and I often use the phrase 'right will come out right' to encourage each other. During a rocky time in our ministry, when some people had left the church and various other unfortunate events occurred, I would ask God why this was happening. 'Surely, if we are in the will of God and doing the right thing, wouldn't He bless that and build His church?' In truth, if we continue to do what is righteous, His righteousness will prevail. Don't dwell on what might be happening in the short term. If you are making righteous decisions, God will bless you and in days, months, and even years to come you will be grateful that you did.

Lord, I don't understand all that is happening, but I do know that You are just and righteous. I trust in You and commit every circumstance into Your hands. You are my righteousness and I hunger and thirst for that to be manifested in me and in Your church. Amen.

September 4th – *Financial Infidelity*

Y1 – Jud 20 & 21 / Y2 – Ezek 33 & 34

Genesis 2:24 (NKJV)
Therefore a man shall leave his father and mother and be joined to his wife, and they shall become one flesh.

Marriage is an act of unity, one which integrates every part of your relationship. However, when there are lies or deceit, it is impossible to become one. We know this is true in the area of sexual infidelity, but a lack of honesty in finances through hiding savings, lying about spending, secret debts, or addictions will be detrimental to any marriage.

When this occurs in a marriage, there are almost always some underlying issues to be resolved. There needs to be some self-examination regarding our lack of wisdom in the Godly stewardship of our finances and spending. We should deeply consider the impact of our actions on our spouse, the fear and worry, we have caused by the financial situation, and perhaps long-lasting insecurities of our breach of trust.

Overcoming mistakes of the past is difficult, and you should seek spiritual help from your pastor. Confessions need to be met with forgiveness, but also an agreed plan for change. Therefore, seek further financial help in making a budget, prioritising debts, and planning agreed spending and saving.

Unity is fundamental in your relationship. You may both feel justified in your actions, but you need to rise above defensiveness in order to deal with the problem. Resentment and anger need to be given to God, whilst you focus on rebuilding confidence, remaining faithful to agreed change of habits, and love.

Working through these issues in a healthy and honest way will open you up to a deeper vulnerability and allow for a new level of intimacy. It can strengthen your bond with one another and give you valuable lessons for overcoming the difficulties of life together. Let the Lord be your comfort and guide.

Father, I bring before you our financial situation. We are struggling and in desperate need of your help, wisdom and direction. Forgive us Father for our poor financial decisions. Please help us to maintain a unified spirit in our marriage and overcome this battle together. Amen.

September 5th – *Push Up*
Y1 – Eph 1 & 2 / Y2 – Ezek 35 & 36

I did a push up today. Well I fell, but then I had to use my arms to get up again, so yes, yes, I did do a push up

1 Timothy 4:8 (NIV)
For physical training is of some value…

When we evaluate the health of men and women in the Bible, their work and day to day tasks were arguably more physical than this generation. They had no cars or public transport, electrical machinery, or technology, but worked with their hands by their own strength. Their diet was organic and unprocessed, far from the reality we live today.

How is your physical health? When was the last time you breathed in fresh air because you went for a walk, and not because you put your head out of a window?

Your health matters. It matters to you, your husband, children, friends, family, and to God. We all pray for a long life that glorifies the Lord, but what if it is cut short because we neglected the very vessel God gave us to use for Him?

1 Corinthians 6:19 (NLT)
Don't you realize that your body is the temple of the Holy Spirit. You do not belong to yourself.

Maintaining a good level of physical fitness will achieve so much more than weight loss. Positive benefits including boosting energy, improving sleep, increasing self-esteem, enhancing immunity, lowering blood pressure, and clearing the mind.

James 1:22 (NKJV)
Be doers of the word.

Whilst we understand that this scripture has much deeper connotations, when taken literally, James is asking us to practice what the Word of God says. In truth, the more physical strength, stamina, and endurance we have, the better doers we become.

Lord Jesus, I recognise the need to look after my body. Help me to understand the importance of physical health. Give me the willpower and vision to break through any barriers that prohibit me, and help me to maintain a consistently healthy lifestyle for Your glory. Amen.

September 6th – *Quick Check*
Y1 – Eph 3 & 4 / Y2 – Ezek 37 & 38

2 John 1:12 (NLT)
I have much more to say to you, but I don't want to do it with paper and ink. For I hope to visit you soon and talk with you face to face. Then our joy will be complete.

I think the use of digital communication makes us more connected than ever, and yet, more disconnected than ever! Don't get me wrong, technology can be incredibly useful in our day-to-day lives; if you need your husband to grab some chocolate from the shop after work you can just send him a text message. Crisis averted! But when we're working with people and building relationships, face to face interaction is essential.

Albeit quick and easy, using technology as the foundation of a friendship is not ideal as it keeps an invisible wall between you; one that keeps you at a comfortable distance. In our text, we see that John understood building real relationships involves time and sacrifice. Though he was elderly and the travel wouldn't have been easy, John made it a priority and told of his plan to sacrifice and go meet his friend in person. *Do you prioritise meeting with people face to face or is it just a quick 'Hey, hope you're okay' text?* The truth is, most of the time, a 'check in' text does not cut it. The caller and recipient simply cannot open up, ask for help, encourage, pray and laugh together.

There is an absolute joy that springs from being connected in a relationship. Conversation over coffee or with another mum at a children's play area is so beneficial to both of you. My challenge to you is to meet up with another pastor's wife. If you live very far away, why not call them or have a virtual meeting via video conference? A text message only gives so much, and how encouraging it would be to know that you have made someone else's day by reaching out! Who knows, they could really need it right now.

September 7th – *God's Daughter*

Y1 – Eph 5 & 6 / Y2 – Ezek 39 & 40

Mark 5:34 (NKJV)
And He said to her, "Daughter, your faith has made you well. Go in peace, and be healed of your affliction."

When I think about the woman in this text, I wonder why was she so afraid when exposed for touching Jesus?[1] We know under Jewish law, she was an outcast, unclean, and shouldn't be in the crowd, let alone touching a holy man.[2] She had endured this affliction for 12 years and spent all her livelihood, suffering at the hands of those who were supposed to help her.

But there is perhaps another reason she was sneaking up on Jesus and trying to keep in the background. Jesus was on His way to the house of Jairus, a well known ruler of the synagogue and an important person in the community. She was unknown and unimportant, being identified only as a 'certain woman.' She wasn't looking for the spotlight, but had faith enough to believe if she could slip in unseen and touch the hem of His garment, it would be enough to bring healing to her life.

Jesus knew exactly who had touched Him, and could have continued walking on, but He took the time to stop. He calls her 'daughter,' the only woman in the New Testament to be called this by Jesus directly. She was of the same value to Jesus as the ruler, and He wanted to give her validation in front of others, not shame her as she feared.

You may feel unimportant and insecure, perhaps from the way you have been treated by others, or past violations that have shaped your view of yourself. This can be as debilitating as any physical affliction. I've had my own struggles in this area, in part because of my upbringing, and although God has brought much healing and restoration, verses like these always bring encouragement.

Jesus sees you as valuable and is concerned with your wellbeing, you are a daughter of God. Have faith to reach out and touch Him.

September 8th – *Testimony*

Y1 – Ps 71 / Y2 – Jer 25

Everything's Wrong by Hannah

Psalm 34:18 (NIV)
The LORD is close to the broken hearted and saves those who are crushed in spirit.

'No he's not!' I said to the policeman, my brain was not yet able to compute that something really awful had happened. I had just been told that my dear brother had taken his own life. It was the lowest point of my life, and it suddenly became very hard to trust that God was there. How could He be when everything around me seemed so wrong and incomprehensible?

In a crisis like this, some questions are never answered. The countless nights spent turning over the unexplainable, 'what if's' and 'should I have.' The blame game can tear you apart. Your emotions are so volatile and can be felt so deeply that it physically hurts. Then there is the sense of detachment from those around you, and you wonder if you will ever feel normal again. There is no easy solution, but here is what I've learned from my heartbreak, to help you with yours.

Don't make decisions based on what you feel.

Remain in the place where God is and He will tend to your wounded heart over time. Give Him time.

Cry out to the Lord with everything you feel.

Recognise that the devil will use your heartbreak and despair to plant his wicked plans of condemnation, unbelief, and lies in order to separate you from God and your destiny.

Read the Word and remember that God remains true even in times of hardship.

Make time to praise and worship Him, for He deserves the glory for who He is, despite our circumstances.

Have godly friends who uplift, encourage, and can speak into your life.

Be encouraged, you will adjust, not by choice but out of necessity. Often you will feel no progress is being made, then realise one day that you've travelled far and can once more say; 'This is the day the Lord has made; We will rejoice and be glad in it.'

September 9th – *Study & Sermon Notes*

Y1 – Ps 72 / Y2 – Jer 26

September 10th – *My Right*

Y1 – Ruth 1 & 2 / Y2 – Ezek 41 & 42

Acts 4:32-33 (NKJV)
All the believers were one in heart and mind …. They shared everything they had … And God's grace was so powerfully at work in them all that there were no needy persons among them.

In our love for Christ and sensitivity to the Holy Spirit, we sometimes sacrifice so other people experience a miracle of God's provision, whether physical or emotional. A person praying for a financial need to be met and God opens our hearts to meet the need. Perhaps someone needs to talk, and you listen … and listen …. and before you know it, you have missed your bus and have to walk home. We can come to view our time, finances, and material things as being *our* possessions. *My* rights.

The healing and deliverance of the man traumatised by evil spirits in Luke 8 always touches me. However I once got to thinking about the owner of the herd of 2,000 pigs.

Luke 8:33-35 (NKJV)
Then the demons went out of the man and entered the swine, and the herd ran violently down the steep place into the lake and drowned. When those who fed them saw what had happened, they fled and told it in the city and in the country. Then they went out to see what had happened, and came to Jesus, and found the man from whom the demons had departed, sitting at the feet of Jesus, clothed and in his right mind. And they were afraid.

I wonder if they were afraid because they had witnessed an extraordinary miracle, or was it because they would have to explain to their boss that his herd was no more. This event caused such a stir in the community. I love the simple phrase that the man was found sitting at the feet of Jesus, clothed and in his right mind. Jesus had healed this tormented, isolated, broken man. Dynamics in the spiritual realm meant the herd-owner's whole business venture, livelihood, wealth and responsibility as an employer crashed around his feet. A sacrifice was made. A life was restored.

As Christian women, we are familiar with sacrifice, but let us retain a right heart. Could God be trying to teach us something? Let us rejoice in a sister or brother's miracle, job promotion or achievement. Let us appreciate the miracle and celebrate with them! The price was paid on the Cross. The Gospel is powerful. We are witnesses to the grace of God's working in the lives of those around us.

September 11th – *Bless You*

Y1 – Ruth 3 & 4 / Y2 – Ezek 43 & 44

Numbers 26:24 (NIV)
The LORD bless you and keep you.

I read this verse recently while feeling overwhelmed by raising children, building a church, and struggling with finances. Blessing means God's favour and protection.[1] God reminded me that His desire was to bless and that I should divert my eyes from what I don't have and proclaim the promise He's given to bless our lives. Take to your hear this wonderful song by Elevation Worship.

The Lord bless you
And keep you
Make His face shine upon you
And be gracious to you
The Lord turn His
Face toward you
And give you peace

May His favour be upon you
And a thousand generations
And your family and your children
And their children, and their children

May His presence go before you
And behind you, and beside you
All around you, and within you
He is with you, He is with you[2]

Genesis 12: 2-3 (NIV)
I will make you into a great nation, and I will bless you; I will make your name great, and you will be a blessing. I will bless those who bless you, and whoever curses you I will curse; and all peoples on earth will be blessed through you.

We are blessed when we are a blessing to others. We should testify of His goodness to others and be a blessing to others in practical ways. Secret Millionaire, the popular, tear-jerker, reality TV programme tracked the lives of millionaires who gave money to people in need, changing the life of both the giver and receiver. *How much more, as children of the living God, can you be a blessing in someone's current circumstance or even eternal destiny?*

Dear Reader,

The following five devotions are a study of the book of Philemon. We studied the Bible as a WattsApp group (because of the COVID-19 lock down). We started out small (Philemon is one chapter long!) and went through the book verse by verse. We got out our concordances, commentaries, dictionaries, translations, transliterations, and the most useful tool of all, our husbands.

The idea of 'study' can be overwhelming and puts some women off, but it is just another word for investigating, giving time to learn about something, inquiring or finding answers to your questions.[i] As we studied, we challenged ourselves, 'What does that mean? How did that happen? Where is this place in the world?' We wrote everything down, prayed, and diligently searched for the truth. Our group discovered a mind transforming depth to His Word and we were all amazed and excited at the insights we received.

Each devotion in this series was written by a different member of the team. Our individual, original notes were extensive, but have been condensed so they are easier to digest. We decided it was important to include this study for the sole purpose of inspiring you to dive into the nitty-gritty of the Word.

We would encourage you to dedicate time for study every week; You will begin to receive the same incredible revelations.

Here are 3 simple tips to help you excavate the Bible

1. Observation: *What does the passage say?* Find out the context by reading the verses before and after to get the entire picture.
2. Interpretation: *What does the passage mean?*
3. Application: *How can you act upon this scripture?* The best way to truly understand the Bible is to live it.[2]

The Word of God is food for the soul and is often very practical. You will develop a firm understanding and personal convictions from it, which will bring both subtle and dramatic changes in your life.

September 12th – *Philemon 1:1-5*

Y1 – 1 Sam 1 & 2 / Y2 – Ezek 45 & 46

This letter is known as a prison epistle, meaning written from prison! *Paul is imprisoned* in Rome, under severe Roman rule. He has sent this letter to Colosse (modern day Turkey). Philemon was one of three men to receive a personal letter from Paul.

Verse 1 This first sentence is likely to be a gentle reminder that Paul is in prison, suffering under the hands of powerful, brutal, and uncompromising men.

Verse 2 Paul addresses Apphia (Philemon's wife), Archippus (Philemon's son), and the church. Paul does this strategically because he wants Philemon to be accountable regarding the request he is about to make. Paul valued Philemon's family and the role they played in supporting their husband/dad by acknowledging them. Families of the minister have valuable roles and are to be a support and blessing to the ministry.

We learn that Philemon conducted church services in his own house and was wealthy. God can and will save those through whom He can bring financial provision to the kingdom. Interestingly, church buildings didn't exist in that time and didn't come about until the second half of the third century.[1] Apphia allowed her husband to have the whole church in her house, which was a huge risk (they were very wealthy).

Verse 3 Paul reminds Philemon that grace is a defining part of our belief system, the means by which we are saved, and that peace is the outflow.

Verse 4-5 Just as we are when we witness conversions, Paul is encouraged to hear about Philemon's faith and the impact he is making. Paul is grateful for this soul and is praying for him by name from his prison cell.

Do you love and appreciate converts in your church? When life seems like a prison-type experience for you, are you still contending for the saints?

Prison didn't limit Paul's ability to make an impact. Neither did it affect his vision for the lost. Prayer was his weapon to fight for these men and women. We can be inspired to do likewise.

September 13th – *Philemon 1:6-10*

Y1 – 1 Sam 3 & 4 / Y2 – Ezek 47 & 48

Paul was in prison yet still cared to inquire about people's personal lives. Growing up I found the English culture can be very polite, but it can feel a little insincere. People may tend to ask how you are doing out of courtesy rather than concern. I've observed other cultures where they ask about your family and personal life with in-depth questions, because they really care. It then allows them to rejoice with you for good things, and to mourn in times of sadness.

Verse 6 Paul had heard about Philemon's faith and what was being achieved through their love for people. His prayer for Philemon is that fruitfulness would abound in his life as he grows in the knowledge of Christ.

Verse 7 The word 'bowels' in the KJV signifies a close personal relationship! God wants us to show one another a genuine love and care from the core of our being. This is what touches people deeply. Prayer is often a big part of this.

Verse 8-10 Paul goes on to request that Philemon puts into action the generosity that comes from his faith. Specifically, Paul is asking Philemon to forgive Onesimus. This is big! However, it's worth noting that Paul doesn't use his position of an aged prisoner of Christ to demand compliance, but instead appeals to Philemon to do it from a position of love. This tells me we should use our power and authority with wisdom and not request more than what is reasonable. Real obedience is from the heart.

I will ask you the same questions these verses caused me to ask myself: *Do you really care for those around you? Do you ask about people from a position of love or only out of politeness? When has your faith last caused you to be generous in how you deal with people?*

Pastor's wives can often feel distant, not integrated, or slightly alien in their congregation. It takes time to build genuine relationships where people can truly know, trust, and enjoy your friendship and vice versa. One thing people can recognise is a heart of love for them, God, the lost and your family. Your open heart and demonstration of love will touch many hearts in ways you may never know but be sure, it can and will make a difference.

September 14th – *Philemon 11-13*

Y1 – 1 Sam 5 & 6 / Y2 – 1 John 1 & 2

God used Paul while he was suffering and in prison. When God's servants are bound, His Word and Spirit are not bound! No matter our situation at present, God can still use us if we allow Him.

Verse 11 Because of salvation, Onesimus has changed and has now become useful. The name Onesimus means profitable, and now lives up to his name.[1]

Through salvation, we can become useful tools for the gospel. *Ask yourself, in what ways am I useful or profitable?*

Verse 12 Paul calls Onesimus 'My own heart' (the KJV uses 'bowels' to signify deep within his being) and is so very dear to him. Paul wanted Philemon to deal gently with Onesimus, his runaway slave. Under Roman law, the slave owner had complete and total control over his slaves and it wasn't unusual for slaves to be killed for much lesser offenses than escaping.[2]

Verse 13 The Good News Bible is very clear, 'I would like to keep him here with me, while I am in prison for the gospel's sake, so that he could help me in your place.' Onesimus had made such an impression on Paul that it was difficult to make the decision to send him back. What a legacy. Onesimus was so useful that he made himself indispensable to the great Apostle Paul. *Could we make such an impression that, hypothetically, it would be difficult to send us away?*

Father, I thank you for the inspiration that Your word brings, cause me to be like Onesimus. I pray that I would be a great help to my husband, children, family, friends, men and women at church, ministry peers and work colleagues. Use me how You will Lord, I am willing. Amen.

September 15th – *Testimony*

Y1 – Ps 73 / Y2 – Jer 27

Speak Again by Anon

It was during an altar call at our annual Harvester's Homecoming conference that I prayed, 'Lord, I don't *need* the preacher to give me a word. I feel okay, have no specific request, and I'm confident in my salvation and relationship with you. However, I would *love* for you to speak to me and give me direction.' The visiting minister asked us to stand and You could feel the presence of God sweep through the building like a fresh wind as we waited with heads bowed and eyes closed before the Lord.

Suddenly, the preacher called me. How did he know my name? Startled, I lifted my head and looked at him.

"Your heart is for your children. You have prayed, 'God please cause my children to have a revelation of You at a young age.' I want to encourage you, that *you* are the key. Your example will cause them to follow Jesus."

Utterly stunned, almost in tears, yet with a smile crossing my face, I couldn't comprehend how those words could be so exact. No one knew my thoughts except for God.

When the pastor spoke those words into my life I was overwhelmed. God chose to speak to me about my children, my heartbeat, and gave me specific direction concerning them. I felt so blessed!

Our God is profoundly personal. He understands our very depths, sees our needs, and knows our longings. God can speak to us anywhere, anyhow, and through anyone. He loves us, that is sure.

September 16th – *Study & Sermon Notes*

Y1 – Ps 74 / Y2 – Jer 28

September 17th – *Philemon 1:14-17*

Y1 – 1 Sam 7 & 8 / Y2 – 1 John 3 & 4

In verse 13, Paul expresses his wish to keep Onesimus with him, so he can minister on Philemon's behalf as Paul is imprisoned. Paul reminds Philemon of his 'chains for the Gospel,' to build up his plea of mercy for Onesimus, who could easily have been put to death for his crime.

Verse 14 Paul respected and valued Philemon and would not act against his will. He wanted Philemon to free Onesimus voluntarily and not out of obligation, because this would demonstrate genuine forgiveness and signify he no longer viewed him as a slave but his brother in Christ.

Verse 15 Paul suggests that Onesimus running away was used by God to bring him to salvation, much like the prodigal son. This was only 'for a season' and now he is returning, because it's the right thing to do.

Verse 16 Paul is levelling the playing field in a sense and demonstrating God's great ability to remove all status within the kingdom by proclaiming that the gospel is for slave and master alike!

Verse 17 When we receive the gift of salvation, we become unified in Jesus. It doesn't matter where you have come from or what you have done, we are automatically accepted into the family of Christ. We know the situation between Philemon and Onesimus is contentious because of the offense, but Paul is asking Philemon to receive him as he would himself.

Do you do the will of God out of love or obligation? Is there someone you need to forgive or welcome back into your life?

We are one body in Christ. Let us never lose the wonder of that.

September 18th – *Philemon 1:18-21*

Y1 – 1 Sam 9 & 10 / Y2 – 1 John 5

Paul requests Philemon to forgive his runaway slave Onesimus, and allow him to serve Christ. Paul had amazing people skills and advised Philemon by encouragement rather than by demand. This is a great trait for any leader. Philemon had the right to put Onesimus to death (he was regarded as his property), but Paul points out they are now brothers in Christ.

Verse 18 Can you imagine the love Paul must have had for Onesimus? He was willing to take the debt of someone else and pay it in full, just as Jesus did for us. Paul is encouraging Philemon to be like Christ.

Verse 19 To emphasise, Paul notes that he himself is writing this, the very one Philemon heard the gospel through. Paul is motivating Philemon to take the next steps in his walk with Christ and highlighted that this is about the next generation.[1]

Verse 20-21 New converts do as much good for us as we do for them. Paul is asking for Philemon to refresh him by granting his request. He is giving Philemon responsibility and has full confidence that Jesus has worked a miracle in him and that he will display true Christian character by going even beyond what he is asking. Paul has undoubtedly instilled this same confidence in Onesimus who is delivering this request for himself.

Ask yourself these questions:
1. Who encouraged your walk with Jesus and do you still pray for them?
2. Who are you encouraging, discipling, and preparing for their destiny in God?
3. Does it bother you if those you have ministered to grow beyond you in fruitfulness?

Lord, thank You for those who have gone before me and discipled me in my relationship with You. Help me to appreciate, love, and pray for those that have invested in my salvation. Give those I am working with a double portion of blessing and responsibility, that their destiny would be fulfilled without hindrance. Help me to keep a righteous and a pure heart in helping others to grow, and not see this as a reduction in my worth. Amen.

September 19th – *Philemon 1:22-25*

Y1 – 1 Sam 11 & 12 / Y2 – Dan 1 & 2

Paul has addressed a major problem concerning Onesimus, who is the runaway slave of Philemon and a recent convert to Christ. Paul challenges Philemon to forgive Onesimus and receive him as a brother in the Lord. This might seem small to us, but slaves were considered personal property and the penalty for a runaway was death. Pauls asks Philemon to treat him with grace, instead of harshness when he returns.

Verse 22 As Paul closes his letter, he hasn't allowed the issue to drive a wedge in the relationship. He's basically saying, 'Hey, do what's right as a Christian. Anyway, moving on, I'd love to come and see you and spend time with you so prepare the guest room.'

There may come a point in friendship where a little confrontation is needed, however, we need not allow that to damage the relationship. Yes, sometimes a relationship can become unhealthy and we should distance ourselves, but most of the time we're talking minor issues! Even in our closest relationships we can experience discord, but we shouldn't be afraid of it or ignore it. We need to value the relationship, and be willing to talk through uncomfortable subjects.

Matthew 18:15 (ESV)
If your brother sins against you, go and tell him his fault, between you and him alone. If he listens to you, you have gained your brother.

Verse 23-25 After dealing with a difficult issue, we should follow up with kindness and communicate friendship even more. Paul sends greetings from others whom Philemon has a relationship with and speaks blessing over his life to reinforce his love.

September 20th – *Many Hands*

Y1 – 1 Sam 13 & 14 / Y2 – Dan 3 & 4

1 Kings 7:13-14 (NKJV)
Now King Solomon sent and brought Huram from Tyre. He was the son of a widow from the tribe of Naphtali, and his father was a man of Tyre, a bronze worker; he was filled with wisdom and understanding and skill in working with all kinds of bronze work. So he came to King Solomon and did all his work.

King Solomon was having God's temple built and brought in a skilled craftsman to make all the bronze objects. The rest of this chapter lists everything Huram made for the temple. King Solomon is famous for the wisdom that God gave him, and here we have it on full display. A part of wisdom is knowing when you need help and not being too proud to ask for it! Solomon knew he needed the finest craftsmen for the project. He was able to delegate and give the job to Huram without feeling slighted or insecure that he couldn't do it himself.

As wives of ministers, it is helpful to recognise the abilities of members in the church, even if it is a skill we have. Why torture people with your cakes when you have real bakers just waiting to be asked? Why exhaust yourself with yet another tea and coffee gathering when others are capable and desiring to serve? Delegation is a wise and a very helpful skill to obtain in itself. It allows men and women the opportunity to serve and have expression in the church. Even if things go wrong, we can all learn, grow, and feel responsible. It also frees us for other things.

Have you learnt the art delegating? If not, why is that? What holds you back?

Children who are raised to embrace responsibility tend to excel in life. Christians mature when they serve. Although we might not see its immediate fruit, when we delegate, ultimately, the whole church grows.

September 21st – *Historical Women*
Y1 – 1 Sam 15 & 16 / Y2 – Dan 5 & 6

Susannah Wesley (1669 – 1742)

Born in 1669, Susanna Annesley was the youngest of 25 children born to Dr. Samuel Annesley and Mary White.[1] Her father was a non-conformist Puritan minister and this influenced her to challenge the establishment, which was unusual in that era. In Susanna's teenage years, she learnt multiple languages and read the works of influential Christian theologians.

At 19, Susanna married the preacher Samuel Wesley and gave birth to 19 children over 21 years, nine of whom died. Her work was never ending. Hand sewn clothes, homemade toiletries, no running water, gardening for sustenance, baking, pickling, preserving, brewing, a state of pregnancy or having just given birth, coping with the deaths of children, yet, in the middle of it all, she was a woman who knew the Lord to the core of her being.

Her children were taught the Lord's Prayer as toddlers and she set aside a time each week for individual religious instruction. Susanna set them up for a bright future in the Lord. Her son John Wesley is known as the father of Methodism and son Charles was one of the leaders of the Methodist movement and a prolific hymn writer.[2]

When her husband Samuel was absent from the home, either in prison for debt or away on church business, Susanna hosted meetings in her home to read a sermon or a good book to further nurture her deep-rooted faith. The meetings began to be attended by neighbours and evolved into the evening service for the church. Although she had no academic acclaim due to a fire that destroyed her notes and literary output, the impact of her life is known today through her diligence to nurture her passionate faith and ability to inspire and offer the gift of salvation to those around her.

September 22nd – *Testimony*

Y1 – Ps 75 / Y2 – Jer 29

Divinely Different by Hannah

Romans 12:2 (NLT)
Don't copy the behaviour and customs of this world, but let God transform you into a new person by changing the way you think. Then you will learn to know God's will for you, which is good and pleasing and perfect.

As a child, it was clear to me that my family was different. I remember watching my mum, a pastor's wife, go about her days full of looking after her family, following up on new converts, and serving the church and thinking how kind and thoughtful she was in comparison to the mums of my friends. I came to realise it was because she had a relationship with Jesus and His light shone through her.

There were times when I would want to be involved in the different things my friends were doing, or want to watch something on the internet, and my parents would rightly not give me permission. I once asked why I wasn't allowed to wear the miniskirt my friend was wearing and my mum emphatically said, 'Because we are different, we are Christians!' and then she graciously explained why. Sinners need to be able to differentiate between the Christian and the non-Christian. All too often we see Christian culture merging into the world's culture. One woman once said, 'I came to church to get away from the world'.

Now that I'm a mother and a pastor's wife, I aim to do exactly the same with my children. I encourage the fact that we are Christians and are to be set apart from the things of this world. Just like my mum, I want the love of God to shine through me for people to see.

Do you try and shy away from this as a parent? Christianity may present challenges for your kids in life, but God will help them to grow and be strong in their faith. Explain to them that being 'different' is a good thing and because Jesus is in us we can be a beacon of hope to the lost.

September 23rd - *Study & Sermon Notes*

Y1 – Ps 76 / Y2 – Jer 30

September 24th – *Going Out*

Y1 – 1 Sam 17/ Y2 – Dan 7 & 8

Matthew 16:18 (NIV)
And I tell you that you are Peter, and on this rock, I will build my church, and the gates of Hades will not overcome it.

Raising disciples and sending couples into the harvest field to pioneer is a vision that the local church should never, ever, lose sight of! I can still hear the shouts of praise and excitement when we announced our most recent church plant.

Having released this couple to their destiny, the preparations moved into high gear. They had to search for a new house, schools for the children, and a building for the church. They visited their new city regularly, built relationships, and scouted out the area whilst learning the culture. These are the practical elements of 'building a church,' but what about the spiritual preparations? One evening on the phone with the wife of this new church plant, we started talking about the logistics of moving to a new house and then the conversation turned to the church. She began to speak about the song leader, worship team, live stream, the nursery, and their new ushers, to which I chuckled and responded, 'But, you don't have a song leader, a nursery to run, or any of these things!' She said, 'I know, but I pray for them like we do!' What a statement!

What is your perspective? Do you pray in that same manner, with vision, faith, and expectation?

Some women go into the harvest field having never felt the fire and burning desire to complete the gospel mission as much as their husband. Instead, they are given to worry, reservations, and a focus on the sacrifice. One thing you must know and remember is that God holds you, your family, and your new church in the palm of His hand and He will build his church.

Adopt the attitude of this faith filled woman and pray with a vision for the unknown to become known.

September 25th – *Unimaginable Heaven*

Y1 – 1 Sam 18 & 19 / Y2 – Dan 9 & 10

Revelation 21:1-4 (NIV)
Then I saw a new heaven and a new earth, for the first heaven and the first earth had passed away, and the sea was no more. And I saw the holy city, new Jerusalem, coming down out of heaven from God, prepared as a bride adorned for her husband. And I heard a loud voice from the throne saying, "Behold, the dwelling place of God is with man. He will dwell with them, and they will be his people, and God himself will be with them as their God. He will wipe away every tear from their eyes, and death shall be no more, neither shall there be mourning, nor crying, nor pain anymore, for the former things have passed away.

This portion of scripture talks about a new heaven and new earth. Heaven can seem so incomprehensible, even when we read the insight given to us in the Bible. Something we do know from this text, and can look forward to, is the dwelling In the presence of and fellowship with God. God will even wipe away the tears from our eyes. The knowledge that this intimacy with God awaits us in heaven and can be an encouragement to all. There is so much more than the things of earth to look forward to.

I Corinthians 2:9 (NLT)
That is what the Scriptures mean when they say, "No eye has seen, no ear has heard, and no mind has imagined what God has prepared for those who love him."

As we run this Christian race, heaven can seem so far away, distant, and unimaginable that we risk losing sight of the finish line. We do not know when Jesus is coming or what the future holds, so we must keep our eyes on Him and be ready at all times.

Lord, help me to keep my eyes focused on you and all that awaits me in eternity and not on the things of this earth. Enable me, so I can help others make heaven their home. Amen.

September 26th – *Keep Adding*

Y1 – 1 Sam 20 & 21 / Y2 – Dan 11 & 12

2 Peter 1:5-9 (NKJV)
But also for this very reason, giving all diligence, add to your faith virtue, to virtue knowledge, to knowledge self-control, to self-control perseverance, to perseverance godliness, to godliness brotherly kindness, and to brotherly kindness love. For if these things are yours and abound, you will be neither barren nor unfruitful in the knowledge of our Lord Jesus Christ.

It would be nice to proclaim we have all of the above qualities, but sad to say, most don't come naturally and must be diligently pursued. God's promise is that if these abound in our lives, we will flourish in the knowledge of our Lord Jesus Christ.

Previous to this verse Peter writes about God having given us exceedingly great and precious promises, so that we can be partakers of His divine nature. This leads on to this this amazing scripture that adjures us to give careful work and great effort [diligence] to adding these qualities to our characters. Why don't we break down the meanings of the list? I have taken all the definitions from the Oxford Learner's Dictionaries.

Virtue: behaviour or attitudes that show high moral standards
Knowledge: the information, understanding and skills that you gain through education or experience
Self-Control: the ability to remain calm and not show your emotions even though you are feeling angry, excited, etc
Perseverance: the quality of continuing to try to achieve a particular aim despite difficulties
Godliness: the fact of living a moral life based on religious principles
Kind (**Brotherly Kindness**): the quality of caring about others; gentle, friendly and generous
Love: a very strong feeling of liking and caring for somebody/something, especially a member of your family or a friend

With these in mind, can I encourage you to dwell on each quality? In the following weeks, just listen to the Holy Spirit bringing things to your mind as you seek to grow in these areas.

2 Peter 1:8 (NIV)
For if you possess these qualities in increasing measure, they will keep you from being ineffective and unproductive in your knowledge of our Lord Jesus Christ.

September 27th – *He's Stronger*

Y1 – 1 Sam 22 & 23 / Y2 – 2 John 1

Sitting at the dinner table one evening, my six year old son and his five year old friend were discussing who was the strongest boy at church. I could tell as I listened that this was a very serious topic of conversation. My son piped up immediately, boasting how he was undoubtedly the strongest. You could see the face of his little friend concentrating hard on how to counteract my son's very bold statement. Finally, he retorted, 'Well, you might be strong, but God is stronger!' My son conceded with an affirmative nod, 'That's true.'

The definition of strength is 'the capacity of an object or substance to withstand great force or pressure.'[1]

The life of a Christian is one that requires great power, endurance, and the ability to withstand force or pressure. *How do we obtain such strength? Is it even possible?*

Philippians 4:13 (NKJV)
I can do all things through Christ who strengthens me.

Since Jesus was a carpenter by trade and in an era without power tools, we can assume He was physically strong. However, the real display of strength was taking on the sins of this entire world at Calvary and defeating hell, death and the grave in the resurrection. This same Jesus lives in us, and through Him we can have the strength to accomplish any task, endure any temptation, and overcome any obstacle. We all have deficiencies, but His power is made perfect in weakness.[2]

Ephesians 6:10 (NIV)
Be strong in the Lord and in his mighty power.

Father, I ask you to forgive me for depending on my own strength. Please give me the stamina, power, and the vision to get through these areas. I look to You Jesus for every answer, knowing that You will strengthen me. I thank You for this provision and by faith I will walk in Your strength from this day forward. Amen.

September 28th – *Honouring Phoebe*

Y1 – 1 Sam 24 & 25 / Y2 – Hosea 1 & 2

Romans 16:1-2 (NKJV)
I commend to you Phoebe our sister, who is a servant of the church in Cenchrea, that you may receive her in the Lord in a manner worthy of the saints, and assist her in whatever business she has need of you; for indeed she has been a helper of many and of myself also.

It is clear from these verses that Phoebe lived up to her name, which means 'radiant' or 'bright,'[1] and was a shining light for Jesus. Cenchrea wasn't far from Corinth, where Paul wrote this letter, and it is likely he entrusted her to deliver it to Rome,[2] deeming her responsible and trustworthy. He also says they should 'assist her in whatever business she has need' and calls her 'our sister,' showing she was a Christian woman whom he held in great honour. Phoebe's name is recorded in the Bible for all eternity.

As a pastor's wife we can be a radiant light, a helper in time of need, a servant of many, and faithful like Phoebe. We think we have to be someone great or do something remarkable, but simple acts of service in obscurity give glory to the Lord. Attending faithfully and listening to your husband preaching is a blessing to him and fulfilling your calling. The smallest acts of service often have the greatest significance. God notices, God remembers, and God rewards!

Hebrews 6:10 (NIV)
God is not unjust; he will not forget your work and the love you have shown him as you have helped his people and continue to help them.

Lord, You have called me to be a faithful servant and a helper in Your church. Help me to embrace responsibility and shine bright like Phoebe so Your name will be magnified. Amen.

September 29th – *Testimony*

Y1 – Ps 77 / Y2 – Jer 31

Salvation Story by Ombline

My childhood was wonderful, we had a great home, good Catholics parents, and everything we needed and more; we were very privileged children.

After some years of living in a third world country where my father had a successful career, we came back to our country. This was a critical time for our family as we faced challenges we had never experienced before. There were financial struggles, and the seemingly great marriage my parents had started to change drastically. My father had multiple affairs. The pillars in my life crumbled slowly but surely, it was a very insecure time in my life. I lived up to the cliché of becoming a rebellious teenager and was permanently in trouble at home and at school. It didn't help that I also had a very difficult time with my studies due to dyslexia. We were uprooted often to follow my dad to his next job assignment. By the age of 15 I had lived in seven different cities and it was tough to make friends over and over again.

It is during this time that I developed severe anorexia and bulimia. I needed to be in charge of at least one thing in my life and I realised I could control my weight. It felt good finally being able to control something, but what started with great hope turned into a nightmare very quickly.

I developed a strong hatred of who I was and what I looked like. I had a recurring dream that I was in a boxing ring trying to fight for my life. I could hear bones breaking, see blood splashing, and when the horror ended, I was left on the floor covered in blood and dying. Then my hidden opponent would turn around and reveal that it was me fighting with myself, to death. I hated to sleep. I thought I was controlling things, but they were controlling me.

I couldn't eat with my family any longer, had to lie to avoid any birthdays or celebrations as they involved food, and I was tormented by suicidal thoughts. I would hear those voices of pure hatred, 'You are worthless, nobody cares, why don't you just kill yourself?'

At 26 years old, I ran away to England hoping I would leave my problems behind me. My eating disorder was so out of control and my body so damaged that I was told by doctors I had become infertile. I had no solutions or accountability!

About this time, I was invited to a church service. I had long lost any faith in God and had become a fervent atheist, however I was so desperate that I decided to give it a try. Even though I did not understand much of what was going on because my English was very poor at the time, when the preacher made a call for those who wanted to receive Jesus Christ, I responded. When we prayed, such a peace washed over me that I broke into tears, something I had not done in years, and I felt the love of God fill the emptiness inside. As I closed my eyes, I saw a hand removing heavy bags off my shoulders and I knew I was free, that there was hope, and I have a life to be lived ahead of me!

On that day 4 May 2008, I was healed and set free from depression, bulimia, anorexia, self-hatred, and suicidal thoughts! I later met and married a wonderful man and together we pioneered a church and are currently missionaries in Africa. The cherry on the cake is that by the grace of God we have four beautiful children. Satan meant to destroy. God has healed and restored me. Praise God for His eternal love, provisions and care for each of His children!

September 30th – *Study & Sermon Notes*

Y1 – Ps 78 / Y2 – Jer 32

Thank you for reading The Devotional Life of a Pastor's Wife

Our prayer is for God to continually stir your heart and give you a fresh ability to minister with effectiveness and joy. But as this volume draws to a close, we are aware that the ministry can take its toll on the best of us. This can sometimes result in a crisis of faith that is difficult to talk about. If you find yourself in this position, we want to reassure you that you belong to a Saviour who loves you today as much as the day you first received Him, and it is possible to start again. Here is a prayer of repentance for the woman whose heart has gone astray.

Father, I come before you today and acknowledge my sin. I repent of all unrighteousness and I am asking you to take lordship over my life and give me the strength to change. I believe that Jesus died and rose again on the third day and in faith I receive your forgiveness and salvation. I surrender my heart and future into your hands. Thank you, in Jesus name, Amen.

We encourage you to speak to your pastor, husband or trusted spiritual friend about the decision you have made today. God's mercies are renewed every day and his love for you endures forever.

BOOK RECOMMENDATIONS

Autobiographical
Bruchko – Bruce Olsen
Chasing the Dragon – Jackie Pullinger
Hungry for More of Jesus– Rev David Wilkerson
Run Baby Run – Nicky Cruz
Seeking Allah, Finding Jesus – Nabeel Qureshi
The Cross and the Switchblade – Rev David Wilkerson
Tramp for the Lord – Corrie Ten Boom

Financial
The Money Secret – Rob Parsons

General
Armed and Dangerous: The Ultimate Battle Plan for Targeting and Defeating the Enemy – John Ramirez
Case for Christ: A Journalist's Personal Investigation of the Evidence for Jesus – Lee Strobel
Deadly Emotions – Don Colbert
Deliverance to Dominion: How to Gain Control of Your Life – John Gooding and Joseph Campbell (Christian Fellowship Ministries)
Disciplines of a Godly Woman – Barbara Hughes
Fresh Wind, Fresh Fire – Dean Merrill and Jim Cymbala
Gay Girl, Good God: The Story of Who I Was, and Who God Has Always Been – Jackie Hill Perry
How to Win Friends and Influence People – Dale Carnegie
Knowing God – J I Packer
Let Me Be A Woman – Elisabeth Elliot
Lies Women Believe and the Truth That Sets Them Free – Nancy Leigh DeMoss
Living a Life of Fire – Reinhard Bonnke
Mere Christianity – C S Lewis
More Than A Carpenter – Josh McDowell and Sean McDowell
Power Through Prayer – E M Bounds
Still Taking The Land – Wayman Mitchell and Greg Mitchell (Christian Fellowship Ministries)
Why Standards? – Jay Nembhard (Christian Fellowship Ministries)

Zeal Without Burnout – Christopher Ash

Marriage
Devine Design: God's Complementary Roles for Men and Women – John F MacArthur
His Needs, Her Needs – Willard F Harley Jr
Sacred Marriage – Gary Thomas
The Legacy of a Couple – Ruth and Billy Graham
The Proper Care and Feeding of Husbands – Dr Laura Schlessinger
The Surrendered Wife: A Step-By-Step Guide to Finding Intimacy, Passion and
It's Not Supposed to be This Way– Lysa Terkeurst

Pastor's Wives
Sacred Privilege: Your Life and Ministry as a Pastor's Wife – Kay Warren
The Minister's Wife: Privileges, Pressures and Pitfalls – Ann Benton and Friends
The Pastor's Wife – Sabina Wurmbrand

Raising Children
Aren't They Lovely When They're Asleep– Ann Benton
Bring up Boys – Dr James Dobson
Bringing up Girls – Dr James Dobson
Dare to Discipline – Dr James Dobson
Glow Kids: How Screen Addiction is Hijacking Our Kids – And How to Break
In Praise of Stay-at-Home Moms – Laura Schlessinger
The Strong Willed Child – Dr James Dobson

CONTACT US
pwdevotional@outlook.com
(Need a friend or want to share your story)

WEBSITE
www.pwdevotion.co.uk
(Free complete Bible in one year/two years PDF)

APPENDIX

July 4th – Made Pure
1. 2020, Cleanse, Websters 1828 Dictionary, accessed 27/06/2020, https://sorabji.com/1828/words/c/cleansing.html

July 5th – Stewarding Time
1. https://biblehub.com/greek/1805.htm
2. https://biblehub.com/thayers/1805.htm#
3. https://quoteinvestigator.com/2018/01/30/busy/

July 6th – Friend in Need
1. John 15:15

July 9th – Shimmering Saint
1. oxford dictionary 28.08.20 definition of sanctified

July 10th – Useful Jael
1. https://www.abarim-publications.com/Meaning/Jael.html

July 11th – Looking Beyond
1. Dictionary.com, 2020, accessed 07/2020 https://www.dictionary.com/browse/compassion
2. https://www.askdifference.com/mercy-vs-compassion

July 19th – Destiny Embraced
1. https://www.oxfordlearnersdictionaries.com/us/definition/english/chosen_2

July 23rd – Our Protector
1. https://www.dictionary.com/browse/stronghold

July 24th – New Normal
1. https://quotefancy.com/quote/1485075/Henry-B-Eyring-If-the-foundation-of-faith-is-not-embedded-in-our-hearts-the-power-to

July 26th – Brownie Blesser
1. https://dictionary.cambridge.org/dictionary/english/invent

July 30th – Jehovah Shalom
1. https://www.christianity.com/wiki/god/what-does-it-mean-that-god-is-jehovah-shalom.html

August 3rd – The Comforter
1. https://www.studylight.org/lexicons/eng/greek/3874.html

August 6th – Fruitful Fear
1. https://www.google.co.uk/amp/s/enduringword.com/bible-commentary/psalm-128/amp/

August 8th – Without Reason
1. https://www.lyrics.com/lyric/3290301/Michael+W.+Smith/Missing+Person
2. https://biblehub.com/commentaries/luke/18-17.htm

August 10th – Embracing Earthquakes
1. https://en.wikipedia.org/wiki/Richter_magnitude_scale
2. Luke 6:46-49

August 1st – Jehovah Jirah
1. Biblestudytools.com, The Lord will Provide, 2020, accessed on 10/11/2020 https://www.biblestudytools.com/bible-study/topical-studies/jehovah-jireh-the-lord-will-provide.html
2. Christianity.com, what does it mean that God is Jehovah Jireh, 2020, accessed 10/11/2020 https://www.christianity.com/wiki/god/what-does-it-mean-that-god-is-jehovah-jireh.html
3. N Stone, Names of God, 2010 edition, page 77

August 11th – Testimony
1. Matthew 16:25
2. John 3:30
3. Matthew 16:24
4. Proverbs 4:23

August 13th – Righteous Oaks
1. Mark 4:19
2. Proverbs 3:6

August 17th – Historical Women
1. https://www.oklahoman.com/article/3066857/ruth-graham-saw-wifes-role-as-a-calling
2. https://www.wral.com/billy-graham-s-daughter-speaks-in-fayetteville/12174988

August 20th – Michael's Response
1. https://biblehub.com/hebrew/959.htm
2. https://www.dictionary.com/browse/piety
3. https://biblehub.com/commentaries/2_samuel/6-22.htm

August 21st – Not Robots
1. Jude 1:23

August 22nd – Immense Influence
1. Daniel 6:1-28

August 28th – Spiritual Assaults
1. 2 Corinthians 10:4-5
2. Ephesians 6:10-18

August 29th – Chain Reaction
1. Matthew 28:18-20

August 30th – Free Will
1. Luke 22:42

August 31st – Beautiful Feet
1. https://www.quora.com/What-are-personal-convictions
2. Proverbs 3:6

September 3rd – Jehovah Tsidkenu
1. https://livingtruth.ca/blogs/devotionals/jehovah-tsidkenu

September 7th – God's Daughter
1. Mark 5:33
2. http://www.scielo.org.za/scielo.php?script=sci_arttext&pid=S2305-08532013000100032

September 10th – Miracle Appreciation
1. Luke 8:35

September 11th – Bless You
1. https://www.lexico.com/en/definition/blessing
2. https://genius.com/Elevation-worship-the-blessing-lyrics

Page 98
1. https://www.merriam-webster.com/dictionary/study
2. https://www.biblestudytools.com/bible-study/tips/3-simple-steps-for-studying-the-bible.html

September 12th – Philemon 1:1-5
1. https://en.wikipedia.org/wiki/Church_(building)

September 13th – Philemon 1:6-10
1. Luke 15:11-32

September 18th – Philemon 1:18-21
1. https://www.workingpreacher.org/preaching.aspx?commentary_id=1767

September 21st – Historical Women
1. https://en.wikipedia.org/wiki/Susanna_Wesley
2. https://en.wikipedia.org/wiki/Charles_Wesley

September 27th – He's Stronger
1. Strength: Oxford Dictionaries entry date 30/08/20
2. 2 Corinthians 12:9

September 28th – Honouring Phoebe
1. https://www.mamanatural.com/baby-names/girls/phoebe/
2. https://en.wikipedia.org/wiki/Phoebe_(biblical_figure)

September 14th – Philemon 11-13
1. https://enduringword.com/bible-commentary/philemon-1/
2. https://en.wikipedia.org/wiki/Slavery_in_ancient_Rome

September 26th – 'To-do' List
1. BibleRef, 2002-2020, accessed 07/2020
    https://www.bibleref.com/2-Peter/1/2-Peter-chapter-1.html

1 Peter 3:18 (NKJV)

But grow in the grace and knowledge of our Lord and Saviour Jesus Christ. To him be glory both now and forever! Amen.

Printed in Dunstable, United Kingdom

64265368R00077